SV
796.54
GOR

ACH 9530

SANTA CRUZ CITY-COUNTY LIBRARY SYSTEM

0000111233276

D0440411

The Joy of

796.54   Gordon, Herb.
GOR
         The joy of family
         camping.

	DATE		

10/99

SANTA CRUZ PUBLIC LIBRARY
Santa Cruz, California

BAKER & TAYLOR

The Joy of Family Camping

Herb Gordon

BURFORD BOOKS

Copyright © 1998 by Herb Gordon.
All Rights Reserved. No part of this book may be reproduced in any manner without the express written consent of the publisher, except in cases of brief excerpts in critical reviews and articles. All inquiries should be addressed to: Burford Books, Inc., P.O. Box 388, Short Hills, NJ 07078.

Printed in the United States of America
Design and composition by Rohani Design, Edmonds, WA

10 9 8 7 6 5 4 3 2
Library of Congress Cataloging-in-Publication Data

Gordon, Herb.
    The joy of family camping / Herb Gordon.
        p. cm.
    Includes index.
    ISBN 1-58080-062-9 (pbk.)
    1. Camping. 2. Family recreation. I. Title.
GV191.7.G67 1998
796.54—dc21   98-11791
                                                                          CIP

Unless noted otherwise, all photographs are by the author.

CONTENTS

PROLOGUE

*"In God's wildness lies the hope of the world
—the great fresh unblighted, unredeemed wilderness."*

John Muir, 1838–1914

We paddled slowly, casually, on a September day when the sky was a glorious blue and the waters of Long Lake, in the heart of New York's fabled Adirondacks, were an endless, shining mirror. There were four of us in an old and battered 18-foot aluminum canoe that had been packed bow to stern with gear and food for our week's wilderness journey. This was our last night. We'd reach our takeout about noon the next day.

My wife, Gail, was paddling bow. Sitting behind her, on a blue waterproof duffel bag, was one of our two sweethearts: four-year-old Rebecca, whose curly red hair gleamed in the sunlight. I was paddling stern, and tucked partway between my legs, sitting on another duffel bag, was the other one, her identical redheaded twin sister, Hilary.

"Look," Gail called out. "Is that the shelter?"

"Where?"

She pointed.

"I think so."

Both the girls started to jump up. "I wanna see." "Me, too."

"Ladies, ladies. Sit down." We swung the canoe to starboard toward an Adirondack shelter, an open-face three-sided log shelter with its characteristic sloping roof, that we spotted between towering trees.

"I don't see anyone else camping there."

"There isn't."

"Good."

The bow scraped onto the sandy shore. Gail jumped out. She pulled the bow farther up the bank, then tucked it between her legs to steady it while our impatient daughters promptly scrambled ashore.

"Run up and put your life jackets in the shelter. Come back and help us unload."

We could have easily carried the gear up by ourselves without the assistance of the excited girls, but this was a family wilderness trip, and we all were involved in the work and the pleasure.

There were a few blueberries on a bush beside the canoe bow. The girls eagerly sought them between carrying whatever they could lift to the shelter.

When everything was stowed inside, we sat on the front of the shelter, facing a fine stone fireplace for outdoor cooking. It pleased me that the last campers had stacked a pile of dead firewood in one corner of the cabin.

"You know, I think it's going to be quite cold tonight. We'd be warmer in our tents," I said. "Would you like to sleep in your own tent?"

"I wanna sleep with Mommy." "I wanna sleep in yours."

Gail said: "No. We'll put up both tents. Your tent and Mommy and Daddy's tent. Just like we always do."

"Me, too," said Hilary. "Me, too," said Rebecca.

"I'll get the gear organized," said Gail.

The girls dragged two tent bags containing identical three-season A-frame tents over to a wide, flat stretch covered with leaves. "Where do you want your tent?" They looked around. "Here," said one. "No, here," said the other, standing a few feet away.

"Maybe we can put the tent up right in the middle. Would that be all right?"

In a sense, the job of placing and erecting the tents was a game—but an important one. We wanted the girls always to feel they were part of both the work and the decision making on our trips, not doing only what they were told to do and then running off to play or look for chipmunks.

Dinner was a two-team affair: Gail and Rebecca shared the cooking; Hilary and Dad were fire, water, and cleanup. Before cooking began, Hilary and I carried two plastic buckets down to the canoe and paddled a short stretch into the lake to fill them. Then she helped gather dried twigs from the ground and piled them up in the fireplace while I schlepped in some dead branches.

"How do we know it's all right to burn these branches?" I asked.

"'Cause we found them on the ground." She watched as I tucked a few shreds of cedar bark under the twigs, lighted them, and topped the burst of fire with some of the kindling from inside the shelter, then added a few chunks of larger branches.

Rebecca's and Mom's dinner included a delicious black bean soup, instant mashed potatoes with wild—but store-bought—mushrooms, and grilled teriyaki-style Spam that had been sliced and marinated for an hour in a mixture of hoisin sauce, soy sauce, minced garlic, and honey. (Gail had sliced the Spam, while Rebecca dropped the pieces in a plastic bag filled with marinade.) For greens we had pieces of celery, which Rebecca washed and put onto a plate on the wooden campfire table sitting beside the fireplace. Dessert was instant chocolate pudding with tiny marshmallows. Rebecca mixed the pudding in a small aluminum pot, then stirred in the marshmallows.

Appetites sharpened by the sweet mountain air, the girls gobbled down twice what they would have eaten for dinner at home.

Before cleanup began, Hilary and I again paddled into the lake to refill the two plastic buckets. The water was for washing and rinsing all the cook- and tableware at the campsite. We carefully carried the dirty water well away from the shore to dump it into a small pit we'd dug.

"Why didn't we just pour it in the lake?" I asked.

"We don't want to get the water dirty."

"That's right."

We all joined in burning and flattening a few tin cans before we tossed them and a couple of dirty pieces of plastic into a garbage bag to carry out with us. Carefully, Hilary and Rebecca stacked the clean ware on the camp table to dry in the night air.

Now the girls walked down to the lake with Mom to help her pull the canoe ashore and tip it over, so it could sleep peacefully through the night. As did the girls, minutes after they were tucked into their tent with abundant goodnight kisses.

"I'm sorry we're going home tomorrow," Gail said. We watched the last few sparks of glowing embers in the fireplace. Once we would have piled on extra wood to enjoy the flames of a campfire before going to bed. Tonight the campfire, in keeping with the conservationist practice of minimizing our impact on the area, was the leftover glow of the cooking fire.

"The stars are so bright."

A shooting star streaked for one brilliant moment.

"A good-luck farewell."

The breezes in the trees were a whispering symphony as we dropped off to sleep.

One unusual incident occurred the next morning as we paddled back to Long Lake village. We stopped for lunch in a small inlet and there, behold, the girls saw from a high point on the bank a canoe half buried by sand under the water. With the girls wading into the shallows to help, all of us finally dug the submerged canoe free to float to the surface. We cleaned it out.

The name of a nearby summer camp was clearly imprinted on the bow. Lunch over, we hooked a rope onto the canoe—the girls sat inside wrapped in their PFDs—and towed it behind us about a mile to the camp. We dragged the canoe ashore and turned it over to a caretaker. He applauded the girls for finding the canoe. He called them heroes. He gave each a candy bar.

On the start of the long drive home the girls kept looking at each other. "We're heroes," they repeated. Then they fell asleep.

In Memoriam

"We do not go to the green woods and crystal waters to rough it, we go to smooth it. We get it rough enough at home."

—The Old Woodsman, "Nessmuk" (George Sears), who wrote about the wilderness in the late 1800s. Author of *Woodcraft,* the first guide to lightweight camping and canoeing, hunting, and fishing ever published.

FOREWORD

*"You must pray that the way be long,
full of adventures and experiences."*

Constantine Peter Cavafy, 1863–1933

A family outdoor adventure can be a wonderful experience, recalled with pleasure and repeated whenever possible.

A family outdoor adventure can also be a disaster, recalled with horror and kept, when possible, from ever happening again.

What accounts for the difference almost inevitably can be summed up in three words:

Preparation!
Knowledge!
Desire!

By way of a single example: Napoleon's pithy observation that an army travels on its stomach is equally applicable to hungry kids—and adults—who can work up unbelievable appetites in the woods. And it's no fortuitous accident that those who enjoy eating healthy and tasty meals in camp do so because of advance preparation at home.

But there is something far more crucial to an exuberant family outing than the quality of the food, or the right equipment and tents and clothing: the spirit of the family itself.

Can adults inexperienced in the out-of-doors who dream of setting up a camp beside a lake, backpacking a mountain trail, canoeing distant waters, or pitching a tent in the snows of winter still create an outing that is a joy for children and themselves? Of course.

All that is required is to have the desire to do so, the knowledge of what's involved, and the proper equipment; then to gather all the kids—whether you're a cheerful, single parent with an only child or an adventurous Mom and Dad with a whole passel of 'em—and go.

Everything you need to know is at your fingertips. Start turning the pages.

Personal Equipment and Outfitting

"O mother
What have I left out
O mother
What have I forgotten"

Allen Ginsberg, 1926–1997

PREPARATION

The way to enjoy the great pleasure of family camping is to follow the Boy Scout motto: Be prepared. That means taking with your family not only all that is necessary in the way of food and material goods, but also an awareness of the joy that comes with a camping experience.

If you're an outdoor family—and even if you're new to back-packing, car camping, canoeing, or camping via bicycle or pack train—most of what you need is probably hanging in a closet or stuffed into a drawer. So before you rush off to buy stuff, shake out the stuff you have, dust it off, and consider whether it's important and in serviceable condition. There will be some things you know you must replace, and some you don't have but can't get along without.

Here is a rundown of the most important items needed by each family or family member. They are listed with only brief comments. For a detailed review of each item, see the appropriate chapters that follow.

Tent: Leftover army shelter halves were never very good tents even when they were new. You will need a tent that is secure in a storm, light enough to carry, and has a built-in floor. Suggestion: Don't borrow one from a friend. It may be inexpensive, but is it a tent that meets your specifications?

Tarp: If you don't own one, go buy.

Sleeping bag: A good bag is light, warm in cold weather, and comfortable. Essential.

Pack: Everyone in the family, from the tiniest to the know-it-alls, should have a truly good backpack. Some kids carry books and papers to school in theirs.

Clothing: First, examine the clothing everyone already owns that can be worn in camp or on the trail. Second, buy.

Boots: Consider what kind of hiking the family will be doing before handing a credit card over to the clerk in the outdoor boot department. Good boots are not inexpensive.

Personal equipment: What goes into your pack is your choice.

Kitchen equipment: What kind of cooking will you be doing?

Portable camp stove: Don't leave home without one.

First-aid kit: The list of suggestions on pages 143–44 may include a couple of things you never thought about.

If you're a novice camping family, take a few easy trips before you plan any major wilderness expeditions. Either go by yourselves or with an outdoor organization that leads camping trips for families. It will quickly become apparent to you that there are some things you must have, some that are pleasant to pack along, and some that only clutter your campsite with nonessentials. Experience will tell you the difference.

PERSONAL EQUIPMENT

Whatever type of outdoor camping you and the family will be doing—read these words of Aesop: "It is thrifty to prepare today for the wants of tomorrow." Everyone, from bouncy youngsters to adults, should have a pack in which to carry personal equipment.

For the wee ones this might include such important items as a favorite doll and toy. What goes along in Mom's and Dad's packs is a more complex story. But for everyone, keep this in mind: Personal equipment in pockets or packs should be reduced to essentials—only those things you truly will need or, oh, well, maybe one little luxury you don't want to leave behind. (Wait until you read about the Koosy-Oonek!) Consider the important ones first.

Knives: Let's start with one of the critical wilderness basics, a knife. In our not-too-distant past, no man ever headed into the wilderness without these four essentials: a gun, sharp ax, knee-high hob-nailed boots, and a knife. Guns are now carried only by hunters. Full-size axes have almost disappeared, along with the hobnailed boots. But every outdoorsperson, from the family camper to the mountain hiker, can find a variety of uses for a good knife. Those new to the outdoors, whether car camping in the beauty of early spring in the Midwest or backpacking through the mountains of Idaho in the fall, rarely start out with a good knife, but I've never met an experienced outdoor traveler who didn't have the best knife he or she could afford. And it was always surgically sharp.

A good knife is not inexpensive, whether it's a clasp knife, a knife in a case, or an elegant "hunting knife" in an artistic sheath with a useless foot-long blade. Probably the most useful length of blade is about 3 inches. This will serve virtually every need for a camper, whether that's slicing a deliciously grilled London broil or cutting a rope in an emergency. An excellent-quality blade will be made of 440-C stainless steel, which is highly resistant to rust and corrosion, with a hardness on the Rockwell scale of C57–59—in other words, a tough steel that will hold a razor-sharp cutting edge. Knives with a single blade are the most popular. However, if you're interested in a Swiss Army knife with gadgets, shop first for the Victorinox, one of the finest made. The Champion model contains 24 tools ranging from screwdrivers to a wire stripper. Among the better-quality single-blade knife manufacturers are Buck, Gerber, Russell, Case, Henkels, and Kabar.

Should children each have a knife of their own? Yes, if the parents are comfortable with the idea. It is essential that a child with her or his own first knife to be given some basic instructions in safe handling and usage. An inexpensive Swiss Army knife with a half-dozen tools and a single blade proved the most attractive to our daughters when they were in their preschool years.

Flashlight: Everyone in the family must have their own flashlights, right down to youngsters old enough to turn off the light when they turn in. Each flashlight should go camping only with fresh batteries, and with a spare set. My light is a miner's-style—in other words, I wear it on my head rather than carry it in my hand. The particular model is a Petzl Mega. It operates on three AA batteries that I carry in a small sack around my neck—not in the light on my head. I use a low-power bulb but also carry a spare high-intensity bulb in case I need its brilliant beam. The batteries will power the low-intensity bulb for about 10 hours, the high-intensity halogen bulb for about 3.

Hanging from a cord inside my tent is a small waterproof Mini-Mag flashlight that operates on two AAA batteries. It keeps me from burning up the batteries in my headlamp when we crawl inside at night.

Compass: One to meet your own specifications. If you'll be helping your children learn to use a map and compass, you may find it helpful to buy similar models for both adults and kids.

Alarm clock: Optional. For the out-of-doors consider a small windup in its own carrying case. It never runs out of battery power.

Matches: Waterproof matches, or a throw-away cigarette lighter carried in a waterproof plastic bag. Matches obviously should be carried only in a mature child's pack. (A tip: If something sticky cannot be cleansed easily, spray it with lighter fluid.)

Thermometer: Why not? A miniature model that can be clipped onto the zipper of a sweater will quickly settle all arguments about how hot or cold it really is.

A plastic bottle with a wide top for easy refilling, or canteen: For drinking in the car, for sipping water when you take a break on the trail, and to have in the tent at night.

TOILET ARTICLES

Towel: Keep it small on an outing.

Washcloth: Optional, though mothers usually want to pack one.

Toothpaste and toothbrush: A fold-up toothbrush in its own case is best. The whole family probably needs only one tube of toothpaste.

Soap: Carry a chunk in a plastic bag. I prefer soap that contains cold cream; it helps prevent chapped hands and faces. Since I shave daily, I also carry a shaving brush in a plastic bag when I'm canoeing, but use my chunk of soap when backpacking. Saves weight.

Perfumes and lotions: Carry these in plastic bottles. Sweet smells may be attractive after a couple of days with nothing more than a brief wipedown. But they attract such outdoor companions as wasps, bees, mosquitoes, and small animals too.

Chapstick.

Sunglasses: Only those that block out ultraviolet light.

Whistle to hang around the neck: It's a great help—*if* you can train your children to blow it only for help in an emergency.

Glasses: You might consider bringing a second pair. Also eyeglass tie-ons keep the glasses from slipping off—especially important for active children as well as adults.

Sunscreen: A minimum sun protection factor of 15 at low altitudes, 25 or more at high altitudes. For children: a minimum of 25 or higher regardless of altitude.

Sanitary napkins or tampons: Even if they're not expecting their period, women should carry a supply of personal hygiene items;

a sudden change in environment or activity may alter the menstrual cycle.

Diapers: If your baby is still in diapers, consider bringing only the "old-fashioned" cloth kind. Waste should be buried; the cloth can be washed out and reused. Carrying enough disposable diapers for a few days may simply not be possible.

Insect repellent: The family may carry a single bottle for everyone, or each member may bring his or her own. Repellent with DEET is not recommended for youngsters. If one repellent does not work, try a different one. Because of body chemistry, a repellent ineffective for one person may be fine for another. A spray is better than a liquid, since you can relatively easily spray clothing as well as skin. And don't forget the socks and pant cuffs, and the insides of shirt cuffs and collars, to prevent invasion by ticks.

Olive oil is also effective to protect yourself against mosquitoes. It does not deter a mosquito from launching an attack, but clogs up her proboscis once she does. (The males do not attack.)

That O.W. "Nessmuk" (he always referred to himself as the Old Woodsman), the author of Woodcraft, the first book in the world (1890s) on lightweight camping, made his own favorite repellent in an era when wilderness travelers brewed their own. I know your children will be delighted not only with how it's concocted, but also how it's used. His recipe:

I have never known it to fail: 3 oz. pine tar, 2 oz. castor oil, 1 oz. pennyroyal oil. Simmer altogether over a slow fire, and bottle for use. You will hardly need more than a 2-oz. vial full in a season. One ounce has lasted me six weeks in the woods. Rub it in thoroughly and liberally at first, and after you have established a good glaze, a little replenish from day to day will be sufficient. And don't fool with soap and towels where insects are plenty. A good safe coat of this varnish grows better the longer it is kept on—and it is cleanly and wholesome. If you get your face or hands crocky or smutty about the camp-fire, wet the corner of your handkerchief and rub it off, not forgetting to apply the varnish at once wherever you have cleaned it off. Last summer I carried a cake of soap and towel in my knapsack through the North Woods for seven weeks' tour, and never used either a single time. When I had established a good glaze on the skin, it was too valuable to be sacrificed for any weak whim connected with soap and water.

The O.W. also said, "It is a soothing and healing application for poisonous bites already received."

BINOCULARS

At the first light of dawn, a bird calls out. Another answers. Awake, you slip out of your tent, pick up your binoculars, and walk toward the shores of the lake. Quietly. You do not want to disturb those sleeping, nor startle the birds in

Mumblety-Peg

Naturally, if children are old enough to have knives, they can be taught by their parents how to play mumblety-peg. This is one of those great games of childhood. In it, if you recall, players first hammer a small peg into a pile of dirt. The harder the ground the better. Players take turns flipping a knife from various positions on their body so the knife lands tip first in the soil . To score a point the knife must stick upright. The loser has to pull out the peg with his or her teeth.

Regardless of what use is made of it, the child's knife, like those of the parents, must always be kept clean and sharp, and be put away after it is used. The blade should be wiped dry with a slightly oily cloth.

the distance. Then, through a light mist, you spot flashing wings. In an instant you point your binoculars toward the birds and catch them close up. What an exciting moment!

A pair of binoculars may not be an essential item of outdoor equipment, but it is an invaluable source of pleasure for the whole family—for spotting birds and animals, for stargazing, and for nature study. Certainly both parents and youngsters don't need to own their own pair; still, one excellent set of binoculars is a superb asset for the entire family. It can be passed back and forth when you, or the kids, spot something exciting.

Binoculars are listed by power and brightness—for example, 7×20, 8×40, or 10×50. The first figure means that you are 7, 8, or 10 times closer than when looking with the naked eye. The second figure is the diameter of the front lens in millimeters.

Essentially, the larger the second figure, the brighter an object will appear. A 7×20 is generally considered the minimum for good field glasses. An 8×35 is even better.

There are several factors to keep in mind when you're buying binoculars: First, be certain they have a central focus—that is, one wheel should bring both lenses into focus at the same time. Second, you also must be able to adjust the lenses for your eyes.

This is done by adjusting the nonfocusing lens to suit one eye, then adjusting the focusing lens to suit the other. IF, or individual focus, models are not recommended.

Buy binoculars only after you have actually tried them. Make certain they are sharp and perfect in every respect. Are they easy to focus? Make buying a pair a family affair. Walk around the store with them hanging from your neck. Decide then if they are comfortable in weight, or too heavy for long hikes or backwoods use. Check on the lens coating. "Fully multicoated" means that all glass surfaces are coated and will admit the greatest amount of light, for a brighter image. The distance that binoculars can be held from the eyes is called eye relief. If you wear glasses, you may want to try on a pair with a longer eye relief. Ask questions while you are still sampling. What about special features? Can they be easily adjusted for your youngster? What is the warranty?

Compare full-size models with compact ones that can slip into your pocket and are very lightweight, but do sacrifice some brightness and field of vision and may be harder to use than larger models. The armored, or rubber-coated, binoculars are the most shock resistant; some are waterproof. If you will be carrying them with you frequently, this might be important.

Where weight is a critical factor—for example, with backpackers—consider a monocular. A fine 8×20 will be almost as expensive as binoculars. However, it is more difficult to focus on an individual objective than binoculars are.

CAMERAS

This section is not for the photo buffs who already know their cameras and equipment. Nor for campers quite satisfied to aim-

and-shoot. Nor for youngsters who love to aim-and-shoot; the best camera for them is one that does precisely that.

But for those who want to go beyond the elemental level of totally automatic photography without spending the thousands of dollars necessary to go top of the line, consider for both yourself and a youngster old enough to understand cameras an automatic that has a manual override (which permits you to choose the f stop or shutter speed in special circumstances) and an interchangeable lens system. (Of course, you and your child could share the same system. Cheaper.)

A camera should be able to go from, say, 35mm to 200mm. For long-distance photography, the larger the lens, the closer the subject will appear. In wide-angle photography, the smaller the minimum opening, the wider the territory that the camera will cover, and the smaller the objects will appear. A 24mm lens covers substantially more than the 35mm. A 400mm brings objects twice as close as a 200mm. With an interchangeable lens system you can use two different lenses for wide angle and distance.

Also, if you have an interchangeable lens system there are two extras you may want to consider. The first is an amplifying extension lens. It fastens directly onto the camera body; then the main lens attaches to the extension. A 2X, or two-power, extension lens will double the power of the main lens (for instance, increase a 100mm to a 200mm). The second is an extension tube, which magnifies the size of the subject for extreme close-ups. The tube attaches to the camera body, and the lens is attached to the tube. It is important if you're buying either extension tubes or extension lenses to understand how they will work with your camera. Not to worry, though; the instruction manual explains it all.

OUTDOOR PHOTOGRAPHY

Bright sunlight does not a great picture make. I was taught this some years back when heading on a backpacking trip with a friend who was a commercial photographer. As we drove toward the camp where we would meet up with several other backpackers before starting a four-day hike on the Appalachian Trail into Pennsylvania, I caught a glimpse of a small lake with a backdrop of a wooded hills.

Slowing down, I said: "It's only one o'clock. We have plenty of time. If you don't mind, I'd like to get a picture of that." I climbed out of the car, focused my camera, took a couple of shots, and climbed back in.

Within a half hour we reached our trailhead campsite and pitched our tent. Another car soon drove up with the other four. We called out greetings. They set up tents.

Around four o'clock, my companion grinned. "Now let's go get that picture. We've got nothing to do for at least an hour."

"What picture?" I was puzzled.

"Shut up. Get in and drive."

We drove back to the precise spot where I had shot the lake and hills a couple of hours earlier.

My companion, his eyes sparkling, said: "Now go shoot it. And, Mr. Photographer, take several shots, from different angles."

I did as I was instructed. When I got back into the car he explained he wanted me to learn for myself how the quality of the light in late afternoon compares to strong sunshine to effect the nature of color photography.

I needn't explain the difference in the photographs. Try it yourself. Shoot an outdoor scene in natural light before 9 or 10 A.M. Then shoot the same scene again at midday, and once more in the late afternoon.

The warmth, the colors, the vibrancy of the scenery will be remarkable in early-morning and late-afternoon light. Your brilliant high-noon shots will be postcard flat in comparison.

For those important pictures, try the rule of three. Snap one picture on automatic, or your programmed setting. Then snap a second one f stop higher than normal, and a third one f stop below normal. Among the three you will find one that is the most appealing. (A professional might shoot three full rolls where you and I shoot three snaps.)

If you shoot slides and you don't already do so, the next time you walk into a camera supply store ask for "professional" Fujichrome or

Kodachrome. It is kept in a refrigerator to retain full color value—never on the open shelves. If you're not certain of the ASA rating, or the professional name of different strengths and styles of slide film, a sales clerk can help.

Finally, if quality is important, take your slides to a lab for developing. For prints, tell the drugstore you want the film developed only by Kodak. It may take a few extra days, but the results will be consistently excellent developing and quality prints.

OUTDOOR CLOTHING

The first essential factors to consider when you're choosing what to wear on a camping journey are the climate where you're going and what you'll be doing there. If your outdoor activities are chiefly undertaken in camp areas during warm and pleasant weather, almost any clothing, from cotton shorts to old sandals, is quite sufficient. When you're going beyond those narrow limits, though, take a second look at the clothing you'll need, starting with bare skin. When dressing for cold weather, follow the layer principle: Carry extra outer garments that can be worn for added warmth, or removed when not needed.

For three- and four-season wear, or when you're active in high altitudes where weather changes can be abrupt and severe, undergarments should always include a set of long johns. In an era when new synthetics are continually invented for use in warm and comfortable undergarments, none have yet proved superior to silk. It's only been around for some 4,000 years. Breathable, lightweight, and remarkably soft, silk's exceptional wicking action helps keep your body warm and dry. In brutally cold weather, you can wear the silk under thermal underwear for added comfort with insignificant weight.

Polypropylene underwear has the same wicking action as pure silk and is widely available in light-, medium-, and heavyweight fabrics both for children and adults. In fact, the only underwear to avoid is any "thermal underwear" made of cotton—which does not wick moisture away from the body and feels cold and clammy when damp.

For cold weather wear pants and shirts made of a warm fabric, such as wool or spun polyester. A zip-neck fleece pullover may be better suited to a child than a shirt.

The next step in layering is a warm vest, advisable for both kids and grown folks. Consider only fleece vests, those made with a down or synthetic filling, or wool vests.

Since up to 50 percent of body heat is lost through the head, a warm, windproof, and rain-resistant cap is a necessity for camp comfort, especially for children. Let them choose their own special, colorful, fun caps for their outdoor jaunts, so you don't get stuck with one hanging in the closet.

Campers must have their own gloves. Mittens are generally the most suitable for the very young. For the older crowd take a look at the shell gloves that can be worn alone or over fleece or liner gloves. Ah, the layer principle again.

Finally comes a light, rain-resistant or rainproof, and wind-proof long-sleeve jacket. This will come in handy both for layering, and to slip into on a cool night in camp.

RAINWEAR

The only members of the outdoor club who should avoid wear-ing ponchos in the rain are canoeists: In an upset, your feet could become entangled in the poncho. Otherwise, these garments are top notch on the trail or for kids splashing around camp. While any poncho can be worn over a pack, providing additional protection to its contents, for trail use look for the backpacking poncho with an extension flap in the back specifically designed to go over the pack.

For full protection when you're wearing a poncho, add a pair of rain pants. These are made of everything from vinyl to nylon coated with polyurethane. They also come in two styles: pants held up by a drawstring, and bib-style with over-the-shoulder straps. The latter are superior when you're active and moving around a lot.

Rain suits—jacket and pants—also come in a great range of materials and styles, from simple vinyl models to designer suits made of Gore-Tex, the waterproof fabric that lets the moisture escape from your body but does not let the rain creep in. Your choice will be based in part upon the style and material you are comfortable with, and the size of your pocketbook.

When you're buying rain gear, always check to ensure that the seams are factory sealed, or use tent seam sealer to seal them at home. Otherwise, they are virtually useless.

> **Holding 'Em Up**
>
> Is there a secret weapon to keep rain pants that fasten around the waist with a silly piece of drawstring from constantly slipping down when you're active? Of course there is. Do what canoeists do: Throw the drawstring away and use a pair of suspenders. Another hint: A poncho can be spread under a tent as a ground cloth or strung up as a small tent shelter in an emergency.

SLEEP

For those families fortunate to escape the harried, hustled, and troubled city to paddle a far river, or hike a hidden trail, what is more comforting than the moment when everyone can slip into a bag and sleep the sleep of the just after a rigorous day? But certainly not when someone twists, turns, or tosses while the stars roll gently across the velvet sky until greeted by the dawn because the sleeping bag was too tight, or cold, and the zipper never worked.

A fine sleeping bag is not the only ingredient necessary for a night of dreams and comfort. But it's damned important for both the weary kids and the tired adults.

Finding the right bag for your comfort—and pocketbook—is not accomplished by darting into a store and accepting the first one the salesperson hands you with the assurance you can do no better. See if you can: Toss a bag on the floor. Crawl into it. Zip it shut. Wiggle your feet. Check out the bag when it is stuffed into its own carrying bag. How much does it weigh? How much space will it take up in your backpack? Ask about guarantees and warranties. What is the manufacturer's suggested "minimum comfort level"? Will you be content with a bag useful only for summer camping? Or do you need a bag that will keep you cozy when a blizzard howls around your tent?

It's prudent not to buy a sleeping bag until you have compared for weight and bulk at least two, preferably three, different brands with the same suggested minimum comfort level. While shopping around, recollect the ancient Mayan adage: "An ounce on your back is a pound on the trail!" And the words of the Inuit sage: "Sleeping bag like blubber on seal. Skinny seal always cold."

COMFORT RATING

Sleeping bags are rated by their manufacturer for their minimum comfort. A summer, fair-weather bag with a total loft of around 4 inches will have a minimum rating of between 40 and 50 degrees F. If you plan to extend your camping season from spring into the fall, look at bags with a larger loft and minimum rating of between 20 and 25 degrees F. A winter camper's bag should have a minimum rating of 10 degrees F or lower, and a loft of at least 6 inches. Unfortunately, cold ratings are not an exact science. One manufacturer may rate its minimums higher or lower than the competitor's. At the same time, your own minimum comfort will depend upon whether you sleep warm at the same time your partner is freezing in a bag with the same loft, what you wear in bed, and even what you had for dinner.

Both kids and parents can lower the comfort rating by putting on dry, wool socks, donning clean, dry underwear, adding a light vest, maybe wearing an old-fashioned nightcap, or even slipping one or two of the small plastic chemical heating pouches skiers carry to warm their hands on snowy slopes into their bag on a chilly night. Indeed, smart parents should carry a few extras for a child who may suffer nighttime cold.

STYLES

Sleeping bags are made in these basic styles: mummy, semi-mummy, semirectangular, and rectangular. A good mummy bag has a boxed foot section. This will keep your feet warm, because the shape helps the filling retain its loft. Matched rectangular and semi-rectangular bags can be joined for the couple that enjoys cuddling.

Sleeping bags today come in a wide range of sizes and shapes. The small camper no longer has to struggle under the excessive

A well designed youngster's sleeping bag by Tough Traveler has a large head-flap extension to protect a child's head. Photo copyright © N. Gold.

weight of an oversize bag, and the strapping giant no longer has to sleep wrapped tighter than a sardine. Different sizes are also available for children.

A few years ago several manufacturers came to the startling conclusion that sleeping bags for adults would be more comfortable if they were designed to take into consideration the difference in physical shape between men and women. Today some design bags that take into account the sex of the sleeper. Among those offering these new gender models are The North Face, Lafuma America, Eastern Mountain Sports, and Sierra Designs. On your shopping expeditions don't forget that every outing goods store doesn't handle all models of sleeping bags, and that clerks sometimes conveniently forget to tell customers which models are not hanging in their stores.

FILLING

The most important element in the warmth:weight ratio of a sleeping bag is the filling. No synthetic has yet been developed that equals better-quality down. However, all down is not created equal.

It's unimportant whether down comes from a northern goose or a Chinese duck. The only critical element is the fill power—how many cubic inches an ounce of down will expand to fill in 24 hours. An ounce of better-quality, 550-fill-power down will expand to fill 550 cubic inches. Top-quality fill power ranges from 600 to 700. The price goes up with the fill power.

Caution: No matter what famous outlet sells it, if the label does not specify the actual fill power, or if it says FILLED WITH PRIME DOWN—which means nothing—hang it back on the rack. Promptly.

Given proper care, down bags will retain their loft twice as long as synthetics. However, synthetic filling is far more popular. The chief reason: the substantially lower price of synthetic bags. Its chief drawbacks: weight and bulk. No synthetic filling can expand, ounce for ounce, to as a high a loft, or be compressed to as small a bundle, as down.

There are differences, though no especially significant ones, among various synthetics. Quallofil, Hollofil II, and Polargard 3D are slightly heavier than LiteLoft, Primaloft, or Polargard High Void, but the latter three do not stand up quite as well.

Makers of synthetics proudly point out that if one of their bags gets wet, it can be wrung out and still maintain its loft; if down gets wet, it turns into wet cloth. To some, this is reason enough not to take a down bag canoeing or when the weather threatens. To them, I answer: Nonsense! I either pack my down bag in a waterproof canoe bag when paddling, or stuff it into a sturdy plastic bag when on the trail. Thirty years. Nary a problem.

To ensure maximum comfort range for any sleeping bag, buy one with a zipper shielded for its full length by a tube baffle to keep out the chill air. An L-shaped zipper that goes from top to bottom and across the feet is easier to pop open on the bottom to stick your feet out on a warm night. Sleeping bags should never have the sewn-through seams of a bedroom comforter, because the seams let in the cold. Different techniques can be used, so only the cheapest bags in the store have such sewn-through seams.

Bag shells generally are made of such fabrics as ripstop nylon, nylon taffeta, ripstop polyester, and polyester taffeta. Ripstop fabrics are somewhat more resistant to tearing than the others. Gore-Tex, which repels water and permits body moisture to escape, has been replaced by DryLoft. Although not waterproof, it is highly resistant to wind and moisture; this is also a characteristic of microfibers, which are breathable and keep out light dampness.

HARD, COLD GROUND

A good sleeping bag offers little protection against either the hardness or the chill of the ground. Once, small air mattresses were in vogue with campers: light, comfortable. One drawback: They provided no insulation against the cold ground. With each breath, and each twist, the warm air next to your body is replaced with cold air from the ground.

Three types of mattresses are in general use today—the firm closed-cell foam, the more comfortable open-cell foam, and foam-filled self-inflating sleeping pads.

Perhaps the kindest thing to be said of the closed-cell pad is that it will provide excellent insulation. Still, it has no "give." Every rock and root will stick into your back. It has no comfort factor. The pads usually range in thickness from ¼ to 1 inch. Closed-cell

A bulky, open cell foam pad alongside the latest in sleeping comfort, a self-inflating Therm-o-Rest mattress. There's no doubt which one today's camper leaves in the basement!

pads are most popular with masochists, high-altitude climbers, and lightweight backpackers.

Open-cell pads are soft and cushy and can be squeezed into a small roll. Their greatest problems are that they are difficult to squinch together and offer no protection against groundwater or dampness.

Self-inflating sleeping pads are a superb cross between the comfort of an air mattress and the warmth of cushy open-cell foam. The unrolled mattress springs into life as soon as the valve stem is open. Sometimes it takes an extra breath or two to make certain the pad is fully inflated. However, blowing into the tube to help the mattress expand is not recommended, because it adds too much moisture to the interior foam; this, in turn, affects its life span. The self-inflating pad is deflated by simply rolling it up. When you're shopping for one, again, go into the store—and lie down on the one you've selected.

All sleeping pads come in a range of sizes. It's helpful to select a self-inflating model that's textured. This keeps the weary sleeper from sliding gently off the pad to the bottom of the tent in the middle of the night.

KID BAGS

Sleeping bags are made for the junior set, but when to start using them is a family decision. Actually, the very young may be quite happy wrapped in warm blankets folded over and held together with large pins.

When it's time to shop for a youngster's bag, look for the same quality features of an adult bag, such as a zipper protected by a draft tube and a water-resistant shell. Yes, there's a strong feeling that such features are a waste of money, because children will outgrow junior bags rather quickly. This is followed by a secret urge to stuff them into inexpensive adult bags. However, those are the very bags that provide the least protection.

Reason number one: It's difficult for a child to keep warm in all that empty space. Number two: Cheap filling doesn't keep a youngster any more comfortable than it does an adult. And number three: Simply seeing their parents in warm, cozy bags is not going to make any kids comfortable at night.

Perhaps the wisest way to begin shopping for a bag for a son or daughter is to consider the lowest temperature you're likely to encounter and buy a bag with a minimum rating of about 10 degrees colder.

The same factors apply to choosing a filling for a junior bag as to an adult model. Down is the top-quality insulation, but remember to buy only down with a minimum fill power of at least 550. Otherwise, all of the widely used and increasingly efficient synthetic fillings will do a credible job of keeping the sleeper comfortable.

Do not buy any bag with a shell material or filling that contains cotton. It will absorb water like a sponge, whether from a bed-wetting accident or moisture in the tent. The only role it has is possibly as a liner sheet in a summer bag. Cotton bags are only for sleepover parties at a friend's house, not for the camper.

All well-made bags have a tube that runs the length of the zipper to keep the chill out. Children's bags usually have a zipper that runs down one side only, not across the bottom. But this is no particular problem.

For cold-weather camping, consider a bag with an insulated draft collar that can be tightened around the neck to keep out drafts, or an attached insulated hood with a drawstring that tightens it around the face.

And remember, as with adult models, never buy a bag with sewn-through seams for the outdoors youngster, either. Every seam is a cold finger running over the body.

Bright, highly visible colors, such as yellows and reds, may be the most suitable for family campers. It's easier to overlook a youngster's dark green bag hanging in the trees than a glowing red one.

KID SLEEPING PADS

Where weight is important, such as on trail hikes, the closed-cell pads are the lightest and provide excellent insulation from the cold ground. They are popular with lightweight young campers.

CARE AND MAINTENANCE

Like all clothing and equipment, sleeping bags need to be cleaned occasionally. But—to protect the life of the filling—not too often. Under normal conditions a bag might not need cleaning until it has been slept in for as many as 90 nights. If you're of more meticulous habit, use a light liner bag to protect the sleeping bag from dirt and sweat. The liner can be washed after every trip. It's like sleeping between clean sheets.

Sleeping Bags

When you're camping, make it a habit to air out your sleeping bags every morning; this dries them thoroughly before they're packed away. Sleeping bags carried all day in a snug pack should be unrolled and spread out as the soon as the tent is staked down. It takes a couple of hours for the stuffing to expand to its fullest. Also, when you're looking for a sleeping bag for a youngster consider buying a good used bag that another child has outgrown. Ask friends. Check thrift shops. Put a notice on a school bulletin board the night the PTA meets.

For bags with synthetic filling, follow the manufacturer's directions for cleaning.

Down bags should never be dry-cleaned. They should be washed gently in cool water, by hand or in a front-loading washing machine. (The agitators in top-loading machines can affect the bag's insulating qualities.) Use only pure soap or the down soap sold at outing stores. Never add bleach.

If you're washing by hand, be careful about lifting the bag up. Carry it in a bundle to avoid putting strain on the seams.

If you're not using a dryer, spread the bag flat to dry out. With a dryer, tumble at a low setting. Tossing a small shoe or tennis ball into the machine to break up any clumps is no longer recommended. Let the dryer do it all.

BOOTS

What type of boot is right for you? Your spouse? The kids?

Consider what type of camping you'll be doing. Will you set up a base camp and take occasional trail trips for a day? Do some serious backpacking? Maybe bicycle from campsite to campsite? Canoe? Once you're clear about where you'll really wear the boots—then, and only then, go shopping. Keep in mind that boots come in both genders.

Boots are designed for various uses. *Backpacker* magazine, in its outstanding "Gear Guide 1997" issue, lists these types of adult boots:

Technical scrambling: These are special lightweight, low-cut shoes for rock climbing.

Trail boots: Primarily low or midcut, trail boots are designed for use on well-kept paths when carrying light to moderate loads. They are made in fabric-and-leather as well as all-leather models; both have multiple seams and flexible soles. Check for quality construction—in particular, sturdy sewing and good traction.

Rough trail boots: Ideal for light backpacking, these boots deliver good support and sole rigidity. The ankle-high uppers should be either leather or a fabric-and-leather combination. Quarter- to half-length steel shanks or semistiff plastic midsoles give these boots enough rigidity to handle bumps and lumps.

Off-trail boots: These boots combine support and flexibility. They have heavy-duty soles and high-traction treads. Look for full-grain leather, above-ankle support, rubber rands for abrasion resistance, and leak protection and minimal seams for best waterproofing.

Mountaineering boots: These are full-grain leather boots that offer ample support for scrambling around on rocks, ice, and snow. They have stiff, aggressive soles with embedded grooves for slipping into crampons. The seamless construction, gusseted tongues, and full rubber rands minimize leakage. The soles should be rockered for hiking comfort.

Double boots: These have a molded plastic outer shell and an insulated inner boot for warmth. Strictly for winter camping and snow mountaineering.

BOOT SHOPPING

Now that you know all the major points of different shoe models, you're still left with a bewildering number to choose from.

Boots for kids come in various designs, from speed-lacing models to those with special soles, all similar to boots made for adults. These "Transcender Juniors" are made by Hi-Tec.

With the foregoing in mind, go shopping—in a well-equipped store with a variety of styles and models. A small number of models on display indicates a store that may be less interested in fully exploring your boot options than in selling what it has on hand.

Discuss the type of hiking you are interested in so the salesperson can help you select the models that meet your special needs.

Your foot should be measured with a Brannock, a device that measures the length, width, and arch of your foot while you're both

A light-weight, low-cut composite boot by Technica made for easy trail hiking (adult model).

sitting down and standing up. The clerk should then inspect your feet with socks off for problems, such as calluses or bone spurs, which may require that adjustments to your boots be made by a boot specialist.

When trying on boots wear the same socks, or combination of socks, that you prefer when on the trail. The boot must feel basically comfortable. Walk around. If possible, walk down a steep incline: Do your toes hit the toe of the boot? Try to wiggle your toes; if they don't move easily you may need a larger size.

Boot companies do not all use the same last. If Brand A just doesn't seem right, try Brand B. This is especially important for women shopping for either hiking or ski boots. Most—not all, but most—

companies now make boots specifically for women from a woman's last, rather than merely marking smaller men's boots as women's, as was the custom for many years.

Don't be swayed by how many different pieces of Gore-Tex, nylon, plastic, synthetics, and leather were cut and sewn to make your boots the coolest ever assembled. Indeed, a full-grain leather boot with minimal seams, whether low cut or high, will be as fine a boot as you can buy for any level of hiking and backpacking.

However, do be swayed by how much those spanking, sparkling boots weigh. The lighter the boot, the happier your feet will be. One pound can turn into a monstrous burden after backpacking 10 miles.

Although a lot is made about how much more ankle support a high-cut boot will give than a low-cut, the reality is that there may not be very much difference. In the only study with which I am familiar, rangers in New York's famed Adirondack Mountains one year summarized all foot and ankle injuries that required medical treatment. They found that half involved people wearing low-cut shoes, street shoes, tennis shoes; the other half involved hikers with sturdy, ankle-high hiking boots.

The widely used Vibram lug sole with its relatively deep grooves has a reputation for providing maximum protection against slippage. However, the newer low-impact lug sole offers equal stability but is far gentler on sensitive wet and muddy terrain.

You can make an educated guess as to how your new boots will feel on your feet on the trail by wearing them at home every night for a week. Arrange for a money-back guarantee if they simply are not the boots for you.

When you finally are satisfied you have the right boots, break them in properly—which means wear them a lot around the house, the yard, and on long walks before they go hiking in the woodlands and over high mountains.

KIDS' BOOTS

While boots for the young set are made of the same materials as those for adults, they usually come in three basic styles: a high boot that goes over the ankle, a medium boot that is only ankle high, and a low-cut, or below-the-ankle, model. High boots are best suited for older, larger children who will be hiking all types of mountain trails both summer and winter. The medium and low types are well suited to less vigorous trails and have a distinct advantage over the bigger boots: They do not weigh as much. Low-cuts pose a problem only for youngsters who splash through every puddle on the trail.

Uppers made of full-grain, split-grain, or nubuk leather are more durable and give better protection than those made of synthetics. However, wet synthetics will dry faster. Not all brands have the same range of sizes. Several begin as small as 10. Children's models usually end at an adult 6.

Buying a boot of appropriate size is a challenge to parents, who recognize how fast kids can outgrow them. Another problem with finding the right size is that if a future hiker sees a pair of those handsome boots on the shelf that he or she has just gotta have, the youngster may not really explain to Mom or Dad fully that they don't feel quite right.

In a proper-fitting youngsters' boot, the heel will be somewhat snug and the toes will have room to wiggle. When the foot is fully in the boot there should be less than ½ inch between the heel and the boot. Test this by putting a finger into the heel of the boot your child is trying on. Also, rub your hands inside the boot to make sure the seams are smooth, not rough.

The more that boots are worn around the house, or racing off to the park, or slinking toward school, the sooner they will be broken in, and the quicker any problems will show up.

Vasque's Kids Klimber boots have a two-layer insole; one layer can be taken out as the feet grow. However, not to be discouraged. You might also try adding insoles to any new boots; they can be removed later to accommodate growing feet.

DRY FEET

Wool or the new synthetics are excellent for outdoor wear, summer or winter, because they will wick away dampness. Cotton socks will not. Some backpackers wear a thin silk or polypropylene liner under wool socks in very cold weather.

Keep your feet dry. On the trail, follow the old military example and take a break every hour. Demonstrate to your children how to help keep their feet happy by slipping off your boots for a few minutes. Rinse out socks every night. With an extra pair or two in each pack, everyone is always assured of clean, dry socks in the morning.

CARE OF ALL BOOTS

Keep them clean. If they don't have an inner waterproof lining, such as one of Gore-Tex, coat them before outings with the water repellent recommended by the manufacturer. When you're treating boots with goo be especially careful to rub it into the seams and where the tops fit onto the soles.

If the boots get wet you and particularly your kids may be tempted to prop them in front of a campfire. Never do this: Too much heat can burn the thread in the seams or even set synthetic tops on fire. Dry them slowly.

BACKPACKS

On rare occasions you may spot backpackers, or canoeists, with all their gear stuffed into a wicker basket without a top. These do add a sense of the bygone days when they were the standard backpack for almost everyone who went into the wilderness. But they are the most uncomfortable backpack ever created. For today's outdoor kids and adults, modern packs are the most comfortable way to carry a heavy load ever devised.

Used Boots

It's often possible to buy used hiking boots for children. Some outing goods stores will accept used boots in good condition as partial payment for a new pair, and resell them at a sharp discount below new boots. (This is equally true of children's skis and ski boots.) Also, look for used hiking boots in thrift shops. If you belong to an outdoor organization you might insert an inexpensive ad seeking boots in the local newsletter or, in turn, offer your child's outgrown boots for sale.

Before You Go Pack Shopping

Whether you're shopping for yourself or an eager young hiker, begin with reality. Since the backpack will be a home away from home, it must be able to hold both securely and as comfortably as possible *everything* that goes with you on the trail.

If you haven't had the experience of trail backpacking and are going shopping for your first pack, it's not a bad idea to lay out on the floor at home all the items you feel you must have—beginning with your sleeping bag, which usually is fastened to the bottom of the pack on the outside, and ending with an extra pair of socks. (P.S.—Include an estimate of the food you'll bring, and a stove.) Estimate the cubic inches or cubic feet these items will fill and keep that figure in mind as only a *rough estimate* of the capacity of the pack you will buy.

If your backpacking will consist of light overnight trips, a bag of 2,500- to 3,000-cubic-inch capacity is usually sufficient. For a long weekend consider something in the 3,500- to 4,000-cubic-inch range. For longer and for cold-weather trips, begin at 4,500 cubic inches and go to as big a monster as you can carry when climbing a steep pitch on an 8,000-foot mountain.

Next, measure your torso. This, rather than your overall height, will determine the size, but not the capacity, of your pack. It's easy enough: Have one of the kids, your spouse, or a friend with friendly hands, measure your spine from the seventh vertebra—that's the knob that sticks out from your neck—to the end point, which also is the shelf of your hip bones. A length of 20 inches allows you a large pack, 18 to 20 a medium, and under 18 a small. Now you're ready to go looking.

Styles

Modern backpacks come in two distinct styles: those with an internal frame and those with an external.

Internal-frame packs have their frame, usually of graphite or aluminum, built into the pack itself. Both the frame and its straps can be adjusted to fit your shape. They carry a load both lower and closer to the back than the external-frame types. Although these packs include padding to protect your back from hard objects, care must be taken to stuff such things as stoves and fuel bottles so they won't dig into you on the trail. These packs are easier to haul around when traveling by car or plane than are external-frame models.

External-frame packs started to go out of fashion in the 1980s but now are undergoing a revival. Several factors account for this. One, by way of an example, is that most models can be adjusted to carry a load at different heights. The highest position puts the pack higher than an internal-frame model can ride, thus enabling you to stand more upright. The frame also has an air space between your back and the pack itself, which adds considerably to the comfort of carrying a heavy load on a hot day. The external-frame pack can also be adjusted to fit.

PACK SHOPPING

In the store, start by loading at least 20 pounds into the backpack of your choice, then slip your arms through the straps. Next, check that the hip belt rides on your hips, not your waist, and that the sternum strap can be adjusted to a comfortable position. Now go walking. Upstairs and down. Around the store. Even if the fit is "perfect," it's advisable to try a similar-style pack made by a different company. The comfort level may be even higher.

Both internal- and external-frame packs come in a variety of styles, ranging from the top-loader whose main compartment opens at the top like a laundry bag to packs that have several main compartments. Virtually all packs have outside pockets for extra storage. Better packs, for both adults and youngsters, have flaps that cover all zippers to keep out the rain. Some also have an over-the-top flap that can be used either to add rain protection to the pack itself or as a cover for gear carried above, and outside, the pack.

SMALL PACKS

Children carrying gear and equipment when they are on the trail must also have packs comfortable for their age and size. This means they should go through the same pack-checkout procedures as Mom or Dad before they leave the store. The sensible recourse for the very youngest is a backpack that is essentially soft, without internal or external frames. A good pack will have compression straps that tighten it so small loads won't bounce around, as well as webbed shoulder straps that run the length of the bag slightly away from the body. Models best suited for light backpacking by children should have padded shoulder straps, back padding, and a padded hip belt.

For the older child, both external- and internal-frame pack systems are available. The external-frame types have one distinct advantage: Their frames can be adjusted as the child grows. This means that successively larger packs can be fastened to the same frame

This "Continental Rucksack" from L.L. Bean is an excellent choice for light loads on casual outings. Courtesy L. L. Bean.

Packs for heavier loads are also available for kids.This one is an internal-frame pack. Courtesy Tough Traveler, *copyright © N. Gold.*

for several years. An external-frame system should be usable for the same youngster from about age 7 or 8 up to 12 years old. By 12, most young outdoor enthusiasts can go into adult pack systems.

Parents whose young are still in the diaper stage can go camping on trips that involve a modest amount of trail walking. Use either a front carrier that nestles your baby in the front of you or the same back carrier popular for carrying children in the city. Some back carriers are designed so that small packs can be tied to the bottom of the frame.

The Weight Factor: How much weight should a child carry? Dr. John Kella, a consultant who advises companies on ergonomics, says youngsters should "try not to carry more than 10 to 15 percent of their body weight" to avoid strain on shoulders, neck, and upper back. Dr. Bernard A. Rawlins, a spine specialist at the Hospital for Special Surgery in Manhattan, says that a pack should always be worn with both arms through the shoulder straps, because this distributes the weight evenly.

As with all expensive items, do make certain you can return an adult or child pack if, after you carry heavy loads around the house in it for a week, you find it doesn't fit comfortably.

LOVING CARE

To ensure that a new pack is reasonably waterproof, seal all the seams with tent seam sealer. I also spray my pack with a water repellent, Silicone Water-Guard, once a year. However, your pack's manufacturer may recommend a different water-resistant spray. You understand, naturally, that in a storm water will still manage to creep in. Thus, everything that must be protected against moisture, including clothing, should be stuffed into tough plastic garbage bags before being shoved into the pack. Stuff in a couple of extra plastic bags along with everything else.

The Gordon Bag System, described on pages 60–64, is as effective for keeping track of gear on a backpacking trek as it is on a canoe or car camping adventure. Use it to divide food and equipment among all the backpackers according to their individual ability to carry weight.

The Tough Traveler child carrier, with a top which can be raised to protect its occupant from sun or rain, is an excellent choice for the backpacking family. Copyright © T. Defrisco.

TENTS AND TARPS

It is not the purchase of quality boots, sturdy packs,

or warm sleeping bags—but of your family tent—that commits you
to the joy and pleasure, as well as the frustration and work, of family
camping.

As with every other type of equipment to enjoy the out-of-
doors, there are no set rules governing what type of tent you must
have. Yours is one that meets your family's needs. No one else's. But
unless you have had the
experience of family camping, some suggestions may
be helpful in what you
choose to spend those dollars on when you're tent
shopping.

Before going into issues
of quality, consider: How
do you plan to camp? For
some families there is no question: A huge family cabin tent, big
enough for 6 or 8 or even 10, with at least two side "bedrooms" and
a common center area, is what they want. On the other end of the
spectrum, there is the family that feels each camper must have his or
her own tiny, one-person tent. The middle ground—and I recommend it—is an individual tent for the parents, and one tent of equal
quality for the children (unless it will take two tents to house the
whole passel).

Reflect for a moment upon what it can be like with everyone
sharing a tent. Litter seems to crop up everywhere. "Hey, I told you
to put this away." "Don't leave that junk lying around." Kids don't
always fall asleep peacefully when they should. And they wake up
and argue. One gets up to pee and the others quickly follow. Parents
who might enjoy a pleasurable moment of their own can only stifle
their desires because, sotto voce: "Ssssh. The kids will hear us."

Waterproof

To ensure that every pack in the family is
waterproof and reasonably secure against
rain or snow, try the under-the-shower
test. Load each pack as you would before
hitting the trail, then hold it under the
shower for a few minutes. Is everything
inside dry when you take it out?

WEIGHT AND BULK

Other points to consider about buying a bulky cabin tent: the
weight, and the effort it'll take to put up. A large cabin tent may

weigh 30 to 40 pounds and take a half hour or longer to erect. Unless someone is willing to schlepp its bulk to that super campsite near the shore, a mile from the car, the tent stays where the car is. And, for sure, no paddlers on a family canoe adventure will permit it in their canoe, either.

Modern self-supporting tents that sleep from two to four adults weigh between 6 and 10 pounds. They can be erected in 10 minutes either for a stay in a campground, or can go anywhere the family wants, whether hiking, biking, or canoeing.

Before they were three years old, we kept our identical red-headed twin daughters in a lightweight, self-supporting, three- to four-person tent with us. However, by the time they reached this advanced age, we felt they should have their own tent. We bought a first-rate two-person tent for them. The first time they slept in their own tent was on a trip to the magnificent wilds of Maine's mountainous Baxter State Park—the northern terminus of the renowned Appalachian Trail. We set up the two tents facing each other, barely far enough apart so that they could still be zipped shut. We explained that one tent would be their bedroom, the other Mom's and Dad's.

Before we tucked them in that first night, with their favorite blankets and toys scattered inside, we had them walk back and forth between the two tents. We went to bed. We called for them to come visit us in the dark. We edged them back to their tent. We visited them a few minutes later. They were asleep. No tears. No fears. In the first light of morning they came bouncing joyfully across the 2 feet separating the tents to crawl into our sleeping bags.

As the giggling, cheerful twins grew older, we placed the tents farther and farther apart. We always let the girls select the distance. Occasionally, especially in doubtful weather, we would put up a tarp and place one tent on each side with only the tent front doors actually under the tarp.

It is as important for the young ones to be warm, comfortable, and dry in their tent as the adults. Don't buy quality for the big people and stuff the little ones into a backyard tent.

TENT SHOPPING

The most popular of today's tents are the self-supporting dome style and the modified A-frame. The dome tents look like large rounded boulders, supported by several flexible poles and covered with a fly. They are simple and quick to erect, divert winds, and shed water. The modified A-frames are the traditional A-shaped tents with a fly and additional support from internal curved end and ridge poles.

Tents, like sleeping bags, come in summer, three-season, and four-season styles. Light tents with only a small fly to cover the upper half are usable in warm and pleasant weather. To the eye, there is not always that much difference between the three-season and four-season models. Generally the fly covering the three-season tent does not come as close to the ground as that of the four-season tent, and does not protect the doorways; on a four-season, the fly can be zipped to cover the tent completely.

Self-supporting tents, the easiest and most popular models for today's campers. They must be pegged down securely . . .

... Or this is the result when the wind comes whistling along!

Some models have front and back doors and a fly with a built-in extension vestibule to protect gear outside the sleeping quarters. Separate extension vestibules also may be attached to some tents.

Why a fly for a tent? The tent canopy is made of an uncoated nylon that allows moisture from your breath and body to escape. The fly is made of a waterproof fabric that keeps out wind, rain, and snow. It sits a couple of inches away from the tent itself. The space acts as a sort of insulating layer, keeping the tent warmer in cold weather and cooler in summer.

Flexible tent poles are made in aluminum, tempered aluminum, tubular fiberglass, solid fiberglass, and carbon fiber. The aluminum, tempered aluminum, and carbon fiber poles have the greatest strength:weight ratio. Fiberglass poles are not recommended.

To judge how well a tent will meet your needs, it's necessary to get inside, lie down, look around, and mumble about how well it will fit all its regular occupants. But do go in with a *sleeping bag* for every occupant. You may settle on the next tent down the row.

Are self-supporting tents fully self-supporting? Yes, sort of. However, after those long poles are put into place, you still need pegs to make sure that the floor is pulled out to its maximum, the fly is properly staked down (if necessary), and the empty tent is secure enough not to get blown into the lake when you and the kids are fishing.

Tents are not fireproof. However, especially when children will be using it, only buy a tent made to government flame-retardant specifications. This must be

Tent Prices

The price range for self-supporting dome tents is quite dramatic. The American Camper Peaked Dome three-person, three-season tent sells for about $70. The Bibler Bombshelter four-person, two-door tent for extreme high-altitude mountaineering is $985. Expect to pay between $125 and $175 for a very good-quality two- to three-person, three-season tent with one door and no vestibule. A superior two- to three-person, four-season tent with two doors and a vestibule attached to the fly will range from $400 to $600. The average weight of three-person self-supporting tents is around 8 pounds.

spelled out either on a tag attached to the tent, or in the brochure that comes with the tent. Treated fabric will catch fire if it comes into contact with direct flame, but it won't burn as quickly as untreated fabric. Another point to consider is the color of the fly. Green may blend in well with the out-of-doors, but this may not be what you want for children who find it far easier to spot that glowing red or multicolored fly when roaming away from camp.

CARE OF YOUR TENT

The first necessity for the proper care of your tent is a larger stuff bag. A new tent comes tightly packaged with all necessary poles and pegs. Once it is used, gets rained on, and picks up a touch of dirt, you may not be able to squeeze it back into the damned stuff bag it came in. So buy a slightly larger one at the same time you buy the tent.

A tent should be set up as soon as you get it home. Have everyone in the family join in the fun. It usually takes a few tries to ensure that the right pole is in its correct position.

Then put on the fly upside down and reseal all seams on the fly and the tent floor. Two thin coats are better than a thick one.

Let the first coat dry thoroughly before you spread on the second. When both coats are dry, turn on the hose and see how well the tent sheds rain. Make it an annual custom to reseal all seams.

While it is traditional to carefully fold a tent the same way each time it is put away, this can create problems along the folds. Instead, manufacturers usually now recommend stuffing it into its carrying bag as you would a sleeping bag.

Protect the bottom of the tent with a plastic ground cloth each time you erect it. The plastic should be a tad smaller than the tent floor. If you bought a slightly larger stuff sack for your tent, you should have no problem keeping this ground cloth, plus tent and poles, in one convenient package.

Shake out and air your tent as soon as you return home.

Never put it away wet.

UV light rays will eventually cause fly fabric to deteriorate. If you have a choice, pitch a tent in the shade of trees. Do not let a tent simply sit out in the sun for long periods.

Tarps

A high-mountain backpacker might find a tarp a totally useless waste of ounces when scrambling up a steep pitch at 10,000 feet. On the other hand, the camping family not only can erect a tarp for protection from a broiling sun but also may find the lack of one a serious problem when rain comes sweeping in just as the cooking is started.

An 11-foot by 11-foot tarp of coated oxford nylon, fully equipped as a dining canopy with four nonadjustable aluminum corner poles and an adjustable center pole, weighs about 15 pounds. This is no problem for the car camper. Where the weight may prove a problem, such as when you're hauling gear, food, and canoes on a portage trail around a stretch of Class V rapids, consider a 10-by-10 tarp of reinforced high-count urethane-coated nylon, with grommets set at the corners and every 3 inches, without poles, and held aloft by ropes tied to trees. It will weigh 2 to 3 pounds.

Camp on a rainy day displaying various forms of shelter—self-supporting tents, the modified A-frame (second from left), and the ever-handy tarp (at right).

We have been using for some years an uncoated 10-by-10 tarp made of Egyptian long staple cotton. Weight: 2 pounds. Not a complaint.

To prevent a tarp tied to trees from turning into a huge basin when it rains, the center must be elevated in some manner, with either a rope ridge pole or a center pole. Long gone are the days when we would chop down a tall sapling for use as a center pole. Now we carry an adjustable aluminum center pole for this single purpose.

An adjustable 8-foot aluminum center pole could be ordered in the late 1990s for about $8 from Texsport, 1332 Conrad Sauer, Houston, TX 77043.

THE KOOSY-OONEK

As careful as even the most experienced outdoorsperson can be to keep track of everything in camp and make certain everything is properly put away at night, occasionally something goes wrong. At the worst possible time and the worst possible place.

Okay, the kids are tucked in their tent. The food bags on the table are covered with a poncho with the pots and pans stacked on top so they will come tumbling down and scare off anything four-footed snooping around for a free night snack.

You're off to bed. Rain in the middle of the night? Not to worry. Everything is properly stowed. No rain on the tent when you awake in the morning. Good. You start slipping into your clothes. But your—oh, no. Yes! Your shoes are outside, each one holding a cup of water.

You know, of course, that you did put your shoes inside the tent. You remember seeing them as you zipped the tent closed. How did they get out there?

The answer is simple: the Koosy-Oonek.

This little-understood camp spook dragged your shoes into the night. He is the same one that spitefully turned on your flashlight after you carefully placed it in your pack, hid your son's hiking socks underneath his tent, and secretly pushed the pot of stew to the edge of the grill so that it would go splashing onto the fire when you accidentally bumped into it.

Be not discouraged. There is something you and the kids can do about this evil genie to keep him from creating problems in your camp, as Horace Kephart explained in his book *Camping and Woodcraft.* He wrote about

> that amusing foible, common to us all, which compels even an experienced woodsman to lug along some pet trifle that he does not need, but which he would be miserable without. The more absurd this trinket is, the more he loves it.
>
> One of my camp-mates for five seasons carried in his "packer" a big chunk of rosin. When asked what it was for, he confessed: "Oh, I'm going to get a fellow to make me a turkey-call some day, and this is to make it 'turk.'"
>
> Mouth-harps, camp-stools, shaving-mugs, alarm-clocks, derringers that nobody could hit anything with, and other such trifles have been known to accompany very practical men who were otherwise in light marching order.
>
> If you have some such thing that you know you can't sleep well without, stow it religiously in your kit. It is your "medi-

cine," your amulet against the spooks and bogies of the woods. It will dispel the Koosy-Oonek. (If you don't know what that means, ask an Eskimo. He may tell you that it means sorcery, witchcraft—and so, no doubt, it does to the children of nature; but to us children of guile it is the spell of that imp who hides our pipes, steals our last match, and brings rain on the just when they want to go fishing.)

No two men have the same "medicine." Mine is a porcelain teacup, minus the handle. It cost me much trouble to find one that would fit snugly inside the metal cup in which I brew my tea. Many's the time it has all but slipped from my fingers and dropped upon a rock; many's the gibe I have suffered for its dear sake. But I do love it. Hot indeed must be the sun, tangled the trail and weary the miles before I forsake thee, O my frail, cool-lipped, but ardent teacup!

So now that you have discovered the secret of how to foil that woodland ghoul, gather the kids around the campfire. Explain to them what you have learned. On your next ramble into the wilds each of you take *that thing* along, no matter who sneers at it, or who giggles about it being in your pack.

It is your amulet. Your medicine. The Koosy-Oonek will never again disturb your family camping adventures by hiding socks or dragging shoes into the rain.

P.S.—And never comment about my camp shaving mirror with the gorgeous color portrait of Queen Victoria on the back, along with a TRiumph 9 0990-style telephone number that went out of service a half century ago.

CHAPTER 2

The Low-Impact Family Camp

*"The clearest way into the Universe
is through a forest wilderness."*

John Muir, 1838–1914

Every half hour or so, as we hiked higher and higher across the cactus- and sagebrush-covered foothills into the forests of Idaho's rugged Bannock Mountains soaring above Pocatello, our Scoutmaster, a slender, cheerful man in his late 20s, would call out for a rest stop.

There were maybe a dozen of us from good ol' Troop 7 on a three-day backpacking trip. Our soft packs were heavily loaded with cans of food, ropes, cooking gear, and spare clothes. Our decrepit military-style pup tents, tarps, and blankets were tied on the outside. It was sheer relief to shed them on our short breaks, all the while mumbling and groaning about our dismal plight.

"Oh, I'm beat."

"Me, too."

"Damn, this pack weighs a ton."

"How much farther we gotta walk?"

The Scoutmaster's jovial voice would call out all too quickly. "Onto your feet, fellows, onto your feet. We only got a couple more miles to go."

Couple? We'd already hiked a hundred. More moans as we slung our packs over our shoulders.

Slowly the vegetation changed. The sagebrush gave way to grasses and juniper trees and soon we were following our Scoutmaster's bobbing butt through stands of pines and aspen. We finally reached our destination, a crystal, icy mountain stream flowing through a clearing.

"Hey, this is it," he said, raising his hand. "Each patrol picks out its own campsite. Find a good place. It'll be home for a couple days."

We scattered, looking for the flattest ground close to the stream to pitch our tents. God, it was great.

A LEARNING EXPERIENCE

Everything we did on that trip was designed to help us become skilled campers and self-reliant adults. But as I look back with today's awareness of intelligent conservation, the entire weekend was a prolonged attack upon the environment.

We ditched our tents, digging deep trenches around them to deflect the rain—if it rained, a rarity in those hot, dry summers. We mercilessly ripped off hundreds of pine branch tips to spread under our blankets so we could sleep more comfortably.

The three patrols had a common menu worked out at a troop meeting the week before. Yet each built its own fire to do its own cooking. Our Scoutmaster even built a small fire for himself so he could cook without interfering with us boys.

In addition to the three-plus cooking fires, we dragged in all the wood we could find to build a huge campfire each night, magnificent but destructive. And we had daily competitions among pairs of Scouts to see which could build a fire from scratch and boil a pot of water first.

Days were spent learning map, compass, and camping skills, and making a variety of camp gadgets out of limbs, saplings, and trees, including a signal tower 10 feet high that could support the weight of one boy, and a crude bridge of trimmed freshly cut logs laid across a narrow section of the stream.

We washed our dishes, and ourselves, in the stream.

We dug a deep pit for a community john, but no one had any hesitation about relieving himself when we were out of the camp and never thought of digging a personal cat hole.

We took turns chopping down a huge Douglas fir with the Scoutmaster's sturdy ax to "learn," and practice, the proper way to fell a tree.

We did bury our garbage, from tin cans to leftover food, in keeping with a rather new wilderness philosophy: "Bash. Burn. Bury." And we made sure each fire was dead out before we shouldered our packs for the long trek home. Marking our camp were blackened stones around each fire ring, the tent ditches, and dozens of broken fresh limbs and tree stumps.

We did not, I must emphasize, destroy the beauty of that mountain meadow deliberately. Camping was a learning experience, and we had a noisy, active, wonderful time doing the learning—in the spirit of those times.

Today, we no longer teach our children to chop, dig, burn, or destroy meadow or tree when we are camping. The whole approach has changed. Now we teach our children to protect the wilderness.

And there is no classroom more pleasant for teaching our children than family camping.

CONSERVATION

Since conservation is based on an understanding of what happens when people destroy the wilds and woodlands, whether by saw, fire, bulldozer, overuse, or carelessness, then it is the responsibility of parents who have this understanding to pass it on to their children.

Personal destruction of the outdoors is not as apparent in commercial or regulated campgrounds as it is in a wilderness area. But wherever you are camping, take a special moment to go for a walk. Explain to children in a casual way the significance of what they see. You and the kids may spot a half-dozen fire sites in one camp area. Question: "Do you think we should make a new place for our fire, or use one of these?"

Only the inconsiderate leave a campfire like this.

Is there a fire ring cluttered with debris? "Maybe we ought to clean this junk up and take it out in our garbage bag."

Point out trees with hatchet marks at the base, or with limbs obviously broken off for firewood. Look for old tent sites marred by ditching. On a trail switchback you will usually find evidence of shortcutting by downhill hikers and mountain bikers. "So what's wrong with this?"

On a large scale, talk about the beauty of the region where you are camping. The hills covered with trees. Or the disappointment while staring angrily at a hill whose trees disappeared in an onslaught of clear-cutting.

Canoe a wild river of clean water, fit for drinking, and tree-lined banks. Why is it such a wonderful place for the family to go paddling? Or a civilized river whose banks are lined with housing and commercial developments, where even fishing is prohibited because of chemical poisoning left by careless industry a half century ago. Or where diligent conservation efforts have cleaned it up so people may again swim in it. Discuss what you have encountered.

Drive to the top of a mountain and either brag about how you can see forever, or make a note of the "mist" from air pollution. Stare in quiet awe at the brilliance of the stars or question why they are so dim. Meditate aloud about the sky and air.

Encourage your children to understand that conservation is everyone's responsibility—from the lone backpacker who hacks at every tree and builds wasteful campfires at night, to the family campers who guard the land and soil where they pitch their tents; the CEO of a mighty manufacturing plant whose chimneys pour pollutants into the air; and the farmers whose careful use of fertilizers no longer pollutes the river that runs past their land.

THE FAMILY CAMP

Where you make camp is largely determined by your method of travel and where you are traveling.

If you're canoeing, backpacking, or mountain biking seldom-traveled areas in forests or desert lands, a satisfactory open space to pitch tents is where you make camp. In well-used areas, such as popular national and state parks and forests, concerned authorities are increasingly restricting camping to campgrounds.

Car campers generally have little choice except to park their automobiles and toss up their tents on regulated campgrounds. These are almost invariably adjacent to lakes and rivers or areas of wilderness beauty. Car campers with off-road vehicles have a far wider choice of where to camp, simply because they have the four-wheel power to drive cross-country. Because of the major damage a single off-road vehicle can inflict on wilderness terrain, however, drivers also have a major responsibility to use their vehicle with wisdom and restraint and not to follow the destructive idiocy of off-road drivers that TV commercials so often glorify. The sensitive off-road driver knows that grinding across small streams or tearing up loose soil on steep hills can cause erosion, damage stream banks, and affect fish habitat. Ruthlessly driving on hiking trails can break down trail edges and degrade the trails themselves.

If you are not certain about camping restrictions, or whether that lonely beach in Basket State Park at the end of a meandering dirt road where you pitched a tent six years ago, close to a year before the youngest was born, is still open to camping, check with the appropriate local authorities. With increasing restrictions on off-trail vehicles, you should also be certain of where you're permitted to take your car in state or national forests or parks. Today's rangers often patrol by helicopter. An illegally parked car may be quite visible from searching eyes above.

When you have the privilege of actually camping wherever you can find a site, whether reached by canoe, bike, foot, horseback, or car, if you're in a virgin area treat it gently. Locate the camp a reasonable distance back from the nearest stream or lake to minimize the likelihood of dirtying the waters. Select a location for your fire that will cause the least damage to ground cover. If the area appeared untouched when you dropped your packs and your butts, let it look that way for the next weary campers.

Where insects are a problem, choose an area partially open to the prevailing breeze if you can. Even a light evening breeze will sweep the little buggers away. Be grateful if a bat or two come whirling through. With their "echolocation" radar they can detect objects as small as a human hair. One hungry bat will gulp down up to 600 mosquitoes and gnats in an hour. And will never touch the hair on you or your children's heads. Indeed, thoughtful adults will point out to their children if bats come flying around that they are helpful friends.

Camping in the open, however, raises some special problems. On one trip we ended our first day's travel by setting up camp on a low bluff. The front of the bluff was a grass-covered open stretch backed by a heavy growth of pine and birch. We pitched four tents completely in the open, but one team located theirs partially inside the trees.

The storm hit about 2 A.M. Wild wind. Bolts of lightning and slashing rain. The scene in the open area was bedlam. A dome tent that had not been pegged was tossed on its side. An A-frame tent was blown down. In the lightning flashes drenched campers hammering in pegs could be seen. The one partially protected tent in the trees suffered no ill effects.

The next night's camp was in a partially open area well protected by trees. Lesson learned.

ESTABLISHING CAMP

Before setting up your camp, encourage the children to search for appropriate tent sites. Avoid camping at the bottom of a hill, where rainwater could come bubbling down in a storm. It is not necessary to trench today's tents, with their built-in water-resistant floors.

Before pitching a tent, clear away chunks of wood, rocks, and twigs. Cover the ground with a plastic cloth a tad smaller than the tent, then pitch the tent on it. The plastic will protect the tent floor from damage.

A good campsite setup. Note the tent is located well away from the metal fire-ring.

Pitch tents well away and upwind from a campfire. Sparks can be carried downwind to burn holes in nearby tents.

Select the most level place possible for each tent. If there is even a slight slope, weary sleepers have a gravitational habit of sliding inch by inch toward the low end of the tent—especially when their heads are not at the high end.

If possible, protect the ground foliage by not erecting tents on grassy spots. The thought of sleeping on hard, dry ground should be of no concern since, of course, each of you is carrying a sleeping pad. Naturally, we no longer clip off the tips of evergreens or rip up local plants to make soft beds for our weary bodies.

When you take down tents, scatter the debris over the ground where they stood.

THE USEFUL TARP

A tarp is a welcome necessity for a family. Shade on a hot day. A roof over your heads in a rain. When you're putting one up, though, beware of letting the center sag. If you don't carry any tarp poles, use one rope as a ridge pole and hang the tarp over it. Fasten the corners to the ground with guy ropes. Precaution: Use TP Signaling Devices, especially at night, to warn unwary campers of the presence of guy ropes. These are simply visible pieces of toilet paper that the kids can fasten to the ropes. TPSDs can also be tied to guy ropes sticking out from tents.

Never use nails as tarp hangers, or as hooks for ropes. Woodspersons, leave those nails and hammers in the camp utility bag reserved for emergencies.

A cord or rope *tied* between two trees makes an excellent line to drape things on, from those wet socks to a sleeping bag airing in the morning sun. But never toss anything—not even a wet handkerchief—onto a tent. Weight on a tent, especially an older one, will strain the seams, causing leaks. Don't get in the habit.

Once upon a few generations ago, a good woodsman would hack, chop, saw, and nail or lash together convenient small trees to shape a worktable area for the cooks. Today, that is anathema.

A tarp erected on its own set of four corner poles and an adjustable center pole.

Wooden tables are common at campsites. If you are a wilderness car or canoe camper you might consider taking along one of those clever roll-up camp tables.

TOILETS

If there are toilet facilities, use them. If not, remain at least 200 feet from the nearest water for personal needs. Dig a cat hole and bury feces and toilet paper under a few inches of dirt.

Some campers suggest that used toilet paper should be stuffed into a plastic bag and carried out with the garbage. This may be acceptable on a one-day trip, but it should be a cause of concern on a junket lasting a week or two. An extremist concept is that campers use stones or leaves in the summer, or snowballs in the winter, as a substitute for toilet paper. This approach left at least one specialist in internal medicine, Dr. Wade Johnson of New York, aghast. His warnings were vehement and simple: The anus could become dangerously infected from dirty stones or leaves, or smeared with painful toxin by anyone who inadvertently grabbed up leaves from poison ivy or poison sumac. As for snowballs, his medical comment was "Brrrrrrr!" Dr. Johnson also suggested that carrying a bag filled with used toilet paper could be "a genuine health hazard. Don't."

Another way to help keep a wilderness site clean is to dig a small cat hole well away from the kitchen area and dump your greasy kitchen water into it. Also, try not to follow the same path every time you walk down to the river for water, so as not to create a trail in the grasses. Wilderness areas are not playgrounds for either the big or little. Wide-field games such as tossing Frisbees, playing catch, or a rousing round of touch football will really chew up delicate turf.

GARBAGE

Exactly what is garbage? To some, it's everything that came in with you that you didn't eat. Everything. Stuff it all into plastic garbage bags and take it out. Leave nothing, as the old saying has it, not even footprints.

However, barring this extreme approach, here are some things to take into consideration.

Bury nothing. No cans. No food. No paper bags. No plastics. Animals will start digging into your garbage pit almost as soon as you are out of sight. Cans and plastics will not decompose for generations. Used plastic bags can be washed out at home and reused.

Drop cans into the fire to burn out leftover contents. Smash them flat with a heavy foot, and stuff them in the garbage bag.

In a well-traveled area, leftover food can be burned or, if not burnable, stuffed into your big plastic garbage bag where all the junk goes, including the empty butane tank for your camp stove. In remote regions bones and food products should be carried well away from camp, out of sight of someone who may come tramping through in a year or two, and left for animals or to rot back into the soil.

Peelings (whether of potatoes or oranges or corn) and leftover vegetables all decompose and enrich the soil. However, if they cannot be disposed of at least a couple of hundred feet from a camp area where they will not be seen, either burn them or carry them out in your garbage bag. It's ugly to walk into a site and find fruit rinds and peelings scattered around. Only thoughtless bums leave such debris.

BREAKING CAMP

It only takes an extra minute or two to leave your campsite clean. Of course the fire is dead out. Have the kids scratch through the ashes to make certain there are no little goodies, such as pieces of aluminum foil or the lid of a can, left behind. If the fire site was built from scratch on fresh ground, cover it with soil and debris.

Who is responsible for camp, garbage, and fire-site cleanup? Naturally, the young ones, as soon as they are old enough. But the parents are responsible for explaining to them why cleanup is a built-in requirement of good camping, along with the garbage sack that follows good campers every day they are in the wilderness.

In well-used sites, do not scatter leftover firewood in the woods. Stack it neatly beside the fire ring. If there is a camp table, stack it underneath.

It is essential with any group, especially one with youngsters, that the last person to leave make a final check of the complete camp area—look down, for anything lying on the ground; look up, for any garments or gear left hanging on trees or draped over bushes.

I can still hear the wild shriek from one mother on a final campsite cleanup. As she walked through she found her son's brand-new sleeping bag hanging on a bush.

THE FAMILY DOG

When the whole family heads off for a wilderness adventure they often include the family dog. But before the kids get too excited about taking the tail-wagger with them the first time, consider what is involved with putting a city dog in an outdoor setting.

There is a small bundle of little problems. Will the dog be permitted in the campgrounds? Most camp areas permit dogs, but they

The family dog makes a welcome addition to the camp, especially for the kids.

must remain on a leash. The American Automobile Association has special books listing campgrounds and motels that do accept animals. Some campgrounds require proof of rabies inoculation. Lacking such proof, are you aware that if your pet takes a nip out of some unsuspecting hand and there is any suspicion of rabies, he may have his head summarily removed and sent to a laboratory for examination? A health certificate and proof of rabies inoculation are mandatory before entering Canada. Mexico requires both, as well as advance approval by a Mexican consul.

When traveling with a dog make certain she wears a metal identification tag at all times. Even a normally placid pet can become excited and leap out of a moving car, or disappear while chasing an imaginary rabbit into the woods. Make frequent stops to give the dog, as well as the kids, the opportunity to stretch, pee, and maybe have a snack.

Your dog's food, if possible, should be the same he is accustomed to at home. A sudden change in diet as well as environment can add diarrhea to any other problems.

The Gaines animal food folks say that a "family dog on a trip needs reassurances from the people he knows and loves. A familiar toy or blanket, sufficient food and water, and frequent roadside stops are all helpful. Strangers, especially children, should be kept at a distance if the dog appears upset. When a dog is nervous, a child's playful poking can provoke even the gentlest animal into growling or snapping."

First aid for a dog in the wilderness usually consists of treating wounds from a confrontation with another dog or a small animal. Wash the wound with a solution of Epsom salts. She'll lick the wound clean if she can reach it with her tongue. A city dog, out of foolish curiosity, may tangle once with a skunk, and once with a porcupine. Never twice. The first sign of a meeting with a porcupine is a howling dog with quills in his nose or cheeks. Unless deeply embedded, these usually can be pulled out by hand, or pushed through the skin into the mouth. In serious cases, take the dog to a vet. Do not let the barbs work their way into the body.

I know of no effective way to rid a dog of the obnoxious odor that marks her only meeting with a skunk. Try dousing her with vinegar or tomato juice. Wash thoroughly. Do not, however, scrub her down with a detergent that contains bleach. Then, until the odor dwindles, tie her downwind from camp.

TICKS AND OTHER PROBLEMS

Ticks are a common nuisance. Examine the dog every night. Simply pull ticks out with tweezers and cover the spot with a dot of antibiotic ointment. Also, hair can become painfully matted from burrs in and around the ears and feet; cut them away with scissors.

Be especially cautious about letting good ol' Fido roam in farm country. Local police officers usually are free to shoot an unchained dog on sight.

If your dog's major activity is going for a walk in the park, or strolling on the backyard lawn, it will become a painful journey for him to hike for two or three days on miles of rough trail with his city-soft feet. He can, of course, be preconditioned to trail walking by going on long walks frequently at home. The sidewalk provides better conditioning than a city park. Although a dog may find them irritating at first and perhaps try to chew them off, doggie booties are nonetheless great protection against sore, torn, and bleeding pads.

Should you have to leave your dog in camp while you go tromping through the woods for a day, chain her. A nervous dog may chew through a leather strap or rope. On the other hand, if she's a sturdy, active dog there's no reason why she cannot share the work, as well as the pleasure, of trail life. Wearing a dog pannier, the equivalent of an adult pack, she can carry her own food—plus some family gear. The pannier should be bright red so no one will mistake Fifi for a dangerous wild animal.

Pack weight, including food and a collapsible bowl, should not exceed one-quarter of a dog's weight, according to Mark Yerkes, director of Urban Programs and Outdoor Leadership with the Appalachian Mountain Club.

Since your dog's bowel movements will be where you and others camp and walk, clean up after him. Campgrounds and trails are not places to decorate with dog droppings.

When you're canoeing with a dog, fasten her in a commercial dog life preserver if there is any danger of her falling into the water on a white-water run, or when you're crossing a large lake. A pannier with small plastic beach balls stuffed in each pocket also is effective as a preserver. Perhaps the greatest danger a canoeist with a dog faces is that at just about the time the nose of the canoe edges into the bank, the dog leaps into the water then welcomes his master ashore with muddy feet and a body wildly shaking off water.

GIARDIA

If you fear your dog may get giardiasis lapping up spring- and stream water, and even puddles, you should relax, according to Dr. Chuck Hibler of CH Diagnostics and Consulting in Fort Collins, Colorado. He says dogs do become infected with the disease; in fact, it's present in almost every dog he's ever examined. At first it may cause a soft stool, but then the dog becomes a carrier without any ill effects.

For her first-aid needs carry pliers or strong tweezers to pull out quills, antibiotic ointment, and the aforementioned Epsom salts to make a solution to wash and treat sores. Always carry a chain leash, a dog muzzle, and the vet's phone number.

The American Red Cross offers both a booklet and classes on pet first aid. Call your local chapter for information.

Suggested reading: *Hiking with Your Dog,* by Gary Hoffman, and *On the Trail with Your Canine Companion* by Cheryl Smith.

CHAPTER 3

Food

"If you can't stand the heat, get out of the kitchen."

President Truman's favorite aphorism

KITCHEN AND CAMP EQUIPMENT

Your back will put up no argument if only one or two light pots are stuffed inside the pack you carry on a backpacking trek for several days. However, if you will be car camping or paddling a couple of canoes down a river on a family trip, weight is of far less consideration. (Until you have to haul the gear on a mile-long portage, of course.) So as it turns out, a "well-equipped" kitchen will depend on how much cooking you will be doing, how you travel, and the foods you serve. First, let's look more closely at the kitchen.

POTS AND PANS

The appropriate pots and pans for your camp kitchen are available in almost every outing store. Consider a nesting set of pots with rounded bottoms—preferably without handles—which pack one inside the other. Rounded bottoms are much easier to clean. Handles tend to break and conduct heat. Use pot grippers. The sturdy Boy Scout pot grippers are far superior to the widely available thin aluminum type.

How many pots will be convenient in your camp kitchen? A backpacking couple who chiefly eat freeze-dried meals in their Sierra cups might well grin at the thought of carrying more than one small pot. But consider what your largest family meal—usually dinner—includes: perhaps soup, a main dish, a carbohydrate, salad, and dessert. The soup, main dish, and carbohydrate generally involve three pots, or two pots and a frying pan. The dessert may need its own pot.

Regardless of the number of pots you prefer, avoid the thin, cheap aluminum type. While they are light, they dent easily and food tends to burn on the bottom. More expensive but far superior and somewhat heavier are spun-aluminum pots, the Sigg Inoxal pots of aluminum-and-stainless composite, and the new nonstick

An inverted canoe makes an ideal food-preparation table.

aluminum pot sets. Sturdiest of all are stainless steel. Your grand-children will take them camping.

For a family, or large group, your largest pot should hold a minimum of a quart of water for each camper.

Select pots with tight-fitting lids. Lids are really not adequate to serve as frying pans—no matter what the catalog or sales clerk implies. For a frying pan, check out Silverstone pans—an aluminum with nonstick interiors—or Coleman nonstick steel pans. Not light, but excellent. If the lids are flat and the pots sturdy you can always place a second pot on top of the first to keep food warm.

If you are considering a Dutch oven, remember the weight. My recommendation is to limit these to car camping or to a horse-packing trip, where a pack horse carries the weight. If you'd like to bake anything from delicious pies to fresh biscuits, check on the light aluminum reflector "ovens." They are usable only with wood fires.

KITCHEN ACCESSORIES

These are the same you use in your home kitchen. For car camping and canoeing, ours include a medium-size wire whisk, metal spatula, long-handled dipper, long-handled fork, can opener, screw-in bottle opener for wine, church key, 1-liter plastic bottle with a wide mouth to use when reconstituting powdered milk or such other purposes as you may devise, aluminum 8-ounce measuring cup, set of aluminum measuring spoons, and sieve to strain out unwanted fly-in guests from the soup pot, along with a vegetable peeler, small oven mitt, and *sharp* kitchen knife. We use a fisherman's filleting knife that fits into a plastic sheath that has a small, built-in sharpener.

For cooking over an open fire, all utensils should have metal handles. Ever seen a melted plastic handle on a fork you accidentally left lying on the grill after checking a piece of broiled chicken teriyaki?

For backpacking, we carefully consider our lightweight meals and reduce the kitchen accessories to meet our menu.

TABLEWARE

For each person, bring one stainless-steel or enamelware cup and large bowl that can double as a plate; and a stainless-steel knife, fork, and spoon. I recommend the stainless-steel Sierra Club–style cups that nest when packed, or hang easily onto a belt when hiking. Be cautious about nonmetal tableware that can melt or burn. To avoid arguments, we paint each person's initials in red fingernail polish on plate and cup.

CAMP GEAR

How much is really needed in the way of general equipment for the camping family? Consider the following, then make your own selection:

For hauling water only in camp I have found one or two 2½-gallon old-fashioned open, collapsible water buckets made of coated nylon or plastic far easier to use than large plastic bottles with tiny spouts, or cooking pots. I also use one 2½-gallon plastic bottle to carry treated water for the whole family while canoeing.

If you carry a central camp lantern, I recommend a model that uses the same fuel you use in your camp stove, and a very light carrying case to protect it. A good carrying case can be made from an old closed-cell sleeping pad. Cut a piece large enough to wrap around the lamp.

At least one camp stove is essential. If you will be cooking over fire, bring a sturdy grill. Either buy one or, as most experienced campers do, use a shelf from an abandoned refrigerator. For a large group, carry two. On a two-week wilderness paddling trip, we accidentally left our grills behind when we pulled away from our first night's put-in. Fortunately, we were canoeing a wilderness river winding through the Precambrian shield country, where shale is abundant. We solved our cooking problem by building either a hunter's or a trench fire and covering it with large pieces of slate where the grills should have been.

For more on stoves and fires see pages 64–76.

Among the most useful implements are a small foldable entrenching shovel or garden trowel, and either a sharp small hatchet or a lightweight fold-up portable saw for preparing deadwood for a fire. Either could also be useful in an emergency.

When canoeing and car camping we carry a larger set of gadgets and instruments than when backpacking or biking. Our complete equipment list includes pliers; two screwdrivers, one regular and the other a Phillips-head; some tacks and sturdy nails, for emergencies only; extra tent pegs; a sewing kit with needles, thread, and, of course, the universally useful safety pins; seam sealer; a package of aluminum foil; waterproof matches; extra mantles for the gas lantern; and a small pair of sturdy scissors with rounded ends.

On all outing trips we carry a few candles whose glow is warm and friendly at the camp table at night, or for use in emergencies, and a candle lantern. The latter is a large plastic tube with an aluminum base in which the candle is placed. I recommend only high-stearate candles, which are almost dripless and don't melt out of shape in a pack on a broiling day. Both these and candle lanterns are available at virtually every store carrying outdoor gear.

Other general items are a spare poncho, which always comes in handy to spread over a woodpile to keep it dry, or on the ground at lunch as a "tablecloth"; the indispensable "mouth bellows"—a ⅜-inch-diameter, 3-inch-long tube to bring a slow-burning fire to instant life; an emergency roll of toilet paper in a sealed plastic bag; a 25-foot coil of 7mm non-flexible rope; a spare *sharp* pocketknife; and the ultimate solution of more problems than anything else—a roll of duct tape. This silver-colored tape can be used to repair almost anything—from sealing leaky seams on a tent to patching a hole burned in a wet shoe propped too close to the fire. We also bring a roll of large, sturdy plastic bags for garbage and such other uses as may occur.

And, finally, the camp 10-by-10 cotton tarp with 15-foot lengths of light rope tied permanently to each corner. On canoe trips we also carry an extension center pole.

THE GORDON BAG SYSTEM

The novices aren't really certain it's all that important.

The experienced campers know.

It is!

Because there really is no adequate way to keep a camp from dissolving into occasional confusion and irritation when everyone, big, little, and midway between, is grubbing through packages and bags looking for a critical item. Of course, it won't show up until tomorrow, and then someone will delight the camp with the creative remark: "I can't believe it was there all the time."

Avoid this by advance organization using the Gordon Bag System. This system is excellent for car camping and canoeing, and can be easily modified for backpacking or biking trips. Basically, it involves three main bags *clearly marked* on the outside—CAMP UTILITY, KITCHEN UTILITY, FOOD UTILITY—along with individual bags for each separate day's meals.

Here is what goes into the various bags:

Kitchen utility: All of the pots, pans, dishes, cups, tableware, and kitchen utensils. Tableware and kitchen tools can each be put into "cloth drawers"—that is, separate smaller bags to make items easier to locate.

If you cook over an open fire, pots and pans will naturally become coated with carbon. Before putting them away, wipe them clean—but do not scrub off the soot. A black pot is far more efficient at absorbing a fire's heat than one with a shiny exterior. When you're putting nesting pots together, separate them with sheets of paper towel or leaves. The pot cluster should be put into a plastic bag before being stuffed into the utility bag. Non-nesting pots should also be stored inside plastic bags to keep the Kitchen Utility bag clean.

Food utility: Drop into it all the ingredients that come out at every meal, such as the coffee, sugar, tea, powdered juices, salt and pepper, a spare envelope or two of powdered milk, perhaps some flour in two sturdy Ziploc bags, herbs and spices, lemon juice, and vinegar. Put all liquids into plastic bottles: Glass breaks.

Camp utility: In go all the general camp equipment that you consider essential, useful, or possible. I would not include in this a spare compass or extra set of maps. If those are essential, they go into the leader's pack.

Food bags: No meal, not even dinner at an elegant four-star restaurant in Rockefeller Center where the appropriate wine is served with each dish, is more delicious than what is served on the plate of a starving camper. To make it far simpler for cooks, whether skilled or novice, to produce that luscious meal in the wilderness, create a food bag for each particular day. First: Each bag contains one day's meals—breakfast, lunch, dinner. Second: Each bag is clearly marked on the outside for which day it is to be used—for instance, Monday, day 3. Wednesday, day 5. Third: In addition to all the food for the three meals, a copy of the day's menu and recipes for each special dish is included.

What goes into the Kitchen Utility Bag for a family of four. Note that the pots nest with rounded bottoms, and the Sierra cups stack up like the plates for packing. Separate pot-grippers are a must to keep fingers from burning.

It all goes into the well marked "Kitchen Utility" bag.

Everything important around a camp site—from a self-contained Optimus 111B gasoline stove to a small broom to sweep out a tent, a rescue rope, and extra tent pegs—goes into the Camp Utility bag.

Some campers fill bags on a different system: All breakfasts in one set of bags, all lunches in a second set, and all dinners in a third. However, I've noticed that putting all the meals for each day into one bag saves windy discussions about which breakfast should be served today.

Loaded Camp Utility bag.

BUYING BAGS

When you're buying camp bags for utility use, consider as a first choice "horizontal" bags with a zipper closure, rather than "vertical" bags, which close with a drawstring or a snap link.

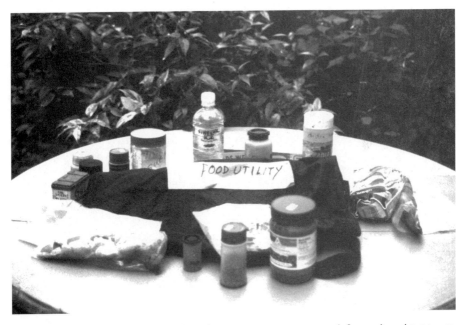

Everything goes into the Food Utility bag that comes out at every meal, from salt and pepper to powder fruit juices. Note that all liquids are carried in plastic bottles.

All camp bags, whether for utility or daily food, are more comfortable to carry if they have shoulder straps. A strap across the bottom of smaller vertical bags reduces the under-the-breath "damnits" because it makes it easier to pull a bag out from under wherever it has been shoved.

Consider what will go into the bags when you settle on the sizes.

When filling the bags, place a tough plastic liner inside every one (except possibly the kitchen utility bag), to protect against water damage.

FIRE

To build, or not to build: that is the question: Whether 'tis nobler to cook over a fire or on a camp stove?

Campfire cooking is becoming an increasingly hot issue between those who advocate using only camp stoves and those who approve of both stoves and the prudent and careful use of wood fires.

The stove-only purists argue vehemently that wood fires are destructive. Even the most careful campers who build them are burning wood and unnecessarily soiling the environment. Camp stoves cause no damage.

But, say the fire builders, wood, unlike oil-based fuels, is a renewable resource. Sensitive campers light only small fires exclusively out of fallen branches and limbs. Trees shed branches year after year after year.

There was a warm, not heated, discussion about stoves and fires when a group of us on a canoe trip on Maine's Allagash Wilderness Waterway sat around one late afternoon, canoes hauled up on the bank, camp organized, and nothing to do for an hour or so except to enjoy the moment.

"Who are the more conservation minded? Fire builders or stove burners?" Ralph asked, smartly grinning because he knew he had touched off a touchy subject.

"Those who only use stoves," came Steve's swift response. "Only."

"No way. Look at it this way. Stoves use fuels made from oil. You agree, don't you, that oil is not a renewable resource? You burn

Pots simmering over a modified hunter's fire made of parallel stone walls. Originally, the walls were foot-thick, 6 foot long, freshly cut logs.

it, it's burned." A slight smirk crossed Ralph's face. "I guess that since the lost resource is pumped up from deep holes far away and you don't see the pumps and you don't see the holes, and you don't even see the oil disappear, it is ignored by you stove advocates."

Hal, another proponent of campfires, added that the fuel and metal that go into manufacturing stoves, gasoline cans, and canisters are further examples of consuming nonrenewable resources by using stoves.

Adding his penny's worth, Steve shot back that too many campers leave dirty pits of ash and blackened stones whenever they build fires in an area without fire pits.

"Damnit, we don't," said Alice.

Since we carried portable stoves as well as built cooking fires, I suggested that both stoves and fires have their appropriate roles in low-impact camping.

THREE CAMPFIRE LAWS

For those who use campfires, there are three laws to follow to conform to low-impact camping.

The first: Build a fire no larger than necessary. It's foolish to stoke up a roaring fire only to heat water for coffee.

The second: When it's lit, put it into service. Don't build it an hour before you need its flickering flames.

The third: Build an efficient fire to conserve fuel.

FIRE TYPES

There are as many ways to build fires as there are campers to light them. Four are basic: the hunter's fire, trench fire, trapper's fire, and Indian fire. Here is how each is built:

Hunter's fire: In the days of seemingly endless forests, the old-timers hauled out their sharp axes and chopped down one or two trees to make two logs about 1 foot thick and 6 feet long. These were placed in a V, a few inches apart at one end and 10 to 15 inches apart at the other, with the V pointed into the prevailing breeze. The fire was lit between the logs, which were then shoved back and forth to whatever width was necessary to support the pots and pans placed atop.

Today, a hunter's fire may be built between two dead logs or, usually, parallel walls of rock (known as a modified hunter's fire) about 12 inches high and only far enough apart to support a grill. The rock walls are aligned with the prevailing breeze. If the breeze becomes too strong, a rock, or slab of wood, can be placed at the windward opening. When breaking camp any smoke-blackened stones or half-burned logs are scattered in the underbrush, and the fire site is covered with ground debris.

Trench fire: This is, in effect, a hunter's fire below ground level. There are times when even the most avid advocate of cooking by fire cannot find rocks or logs. The solution is to dig a trench 2 to 3 feet long and 1 foot deep, with one sloping end so wood may be fed into the fire, and only wide enough to support a grill. Pile the dirt from the trench to one side.

When breaking camp shovel the dirt back into the pit and scatter ground debris on top.

Trapper's fire: This is a combination fireplace and cooking fire popular with hunters and fishermen of a bygone era who expected to be in the same camp for several days. It consists of a back wall 5 to 6 feet high, made of stones or green logs a foot thick, and slanting slightly backward. The fire in front of the back wall is used for cooking, then kept burning through the night to reflect heat into a lean-to directly in front of the blaze.

Indian fire: A common Native American technique was to build a fire and surround it with long branches placed in a pattern of spokes radiating from a wheel. As the wood was burned, the branches were pushed into the flaming center. These fires were kept small, not because the Natives faced any shortage of fuel but rather because of the sacred concept of minimal impact on the environment, whether hunting buffalo, catching fish, or burning wood.

Pioneers had a saying about these small fires that they attributed to the Native Americans: "Indian smart. Build small fire. Sit close. Cook. Stay warm. Paleface fool. Build big fire. No get close. No keep warm. Waste wood." Even if apocryphal it was, and remains, true.

EFFICIENT FIRE

The least-efficient, but by far the most popular, of all cooking fires are those built in the open with the cooking done on self-supporting grills with legs. Nothing blocks the tiniest wisp of wind from blowing away the direct heat of the flames and cooling the pan bottoms, which reduces the full effect of radiant heat.

The most efficient are the hunter's and trench fires, which concentrate reflected heat on the cooking pans. On one of my national Sierra Club canoe trips in the Canadian wilderness trips, a physicist paddling with us, after pondering the fact that at every camp we hunted up stones and built cooking fires hunter-style, sagely observed that "these fires are probably 25 to 50 percent more efficient than open fires." Conclusion: It was worth the effort it took to build them.

MAKING A FIRE

Starting a fire is as elemental as piling a layer of small sticks and branches on top of something that will burn, and striking a match. That "something" is called tinder.

One excellent material is the thin outer bark of birch trees. It has a high oil content and, wet or dry, bursts quickly into flame. Since losing its outer bark does not affect the tree's vital cambium layer, you can have the youngsters shred off as much as you want without damaging it. But bark scrap on fallen branches is also excellent.

The pitch oozing from pine trees also is filled with natural oils and burns readily. Dry dead leaves will make an acceptable tinder, as will a handful of the thinnest of dead twigs. If tinder is scarce, a few wads of toilet paper make a tolerable substitute. Don't be wasteful. You may regret it.

Cover the tinder carefully with a large handful of shreds of wood whittled from a dead branch, or more tiny twigs. Next, place larger twigs atop the pile, either tepee- or log-cabin-style, topped with thumb-size branches. Keep the wood well spaced so air can easily get into the fire. Next—light it. Hmmm, that's the technique I learned on Boy Scout camping trips.

There are two popular methods for helping a struggling fire burst into cheerful flame: A. Crouch down and blow your lungs out. B. Fan it with a hat or frying pan. Both A and B are, bluntly, lousy.

Better is to try the old Native American technique. Natives used a hollow reed. In case you can't find one, carry a 3-foot length of ¼- or ⅜-inch-diameter rubber or plastic tubing when you're camping. To put the flame back in the fire, stick one end in your mouth, and hold the other close to the hot coals or struggling flame. A few hearty puffs and voilà! It's burning bright.

EVENING CAMPFIRES

Yes, a billowing fire glowing in the dark is a comforting sight. Sitting around it, campers draw close to each other—though the intense heat may drive them well back from the flames. Stories are spun. Poems are read. Jokes jump back and forth. Someone is always willing to reach over and grab a few more large chunks of wood and toss them on.

However, in today's conservation-oriented world, low-impact campers keep that fire small. The quiet charm of the evening is as much in the mind of the beholder when staring hypnotically into a small fire as a roaring flame. Some low-impact campers will not build a fire at night at all; they take comfort in watching the flame of a flickering candle. To keep the tiny flame alive, they place the candle in an efficient Plexiglas candle lantern.

To make sure you have dry wood to start the morning fire, toss a few dry branches into your tent when you crawl in for the night, or place the kindling under the plastic tarp that covers the food supply.

FIREWOOD

When it was considered fit and proper to build a fire only with kindling you chopped yourself, the type of wood you used not only determined how long it would burn but also affected the flavor of broiled foods. Today, however, when we make our fires out of fallen branches, we have little choice in how long the pieces of wood burn, or their flavor on broiled foods.

When Horace Kephart wrote his book on camping he compared how easily various woods were to light, how long they burned, and the heat they threw off. Here is his advice for campers:

> Best of all firewood is hickory, green or dry. It makes a hot fire, but lasts a long time, burning down to a bed of hard coals that keep up an even, generous heat for hours. . . . Following hickory, in fuel value, are the chestnut oak, overcup, post, and basket oaks, pecan, the horn beams (ironwood) and dogwood. The latter burns finally to a beautiful white ash that is characteristic; apple wood does the same. . . . All of the birches are good fuel, ranking in about this order: black, yellow, red, paper,

and white. Sugar maple was the favorite fuel of our old-time hunters and surveyors because it ignites easily, burns with a clear, steady flame, and leaves good coal; but it is too valuable a tree, nowadays, to be cast into fire. . . .

Locust is a good, lasting fuel; it is easy to cut, and, when green splits fairly well. . . . Mulberry has similar qualities. The best of the oaks for fuel, especially when green, is white oak.

Most of the softwoods are good only for kindling, or for quick cooking fires. . . . The best green softwoods for fuel are white birch, paper birch, soft maple, cottonwood, and quaking aspen. For a cooking fire that will burn quickly to coals, without smoke, the bark of dead hemlock, hickory, pine or sugar maple cannot be excelled.

Kephart never questioned the fact that everyone bound for the green woods and crystal streams knew well the trees of the forests. We may not practice the art of woodsmanship in chopping down trees for firewood today, but it would help each of us to take more delight in our woodlands if we learned to recognize the trees.

There are as many excellent books on identifying trees as there are on mushrooms or birds. On your next trek, why not carry one? Hey, you may come home smarter than when you left.

CHARCOAL

Car campers (and backyard gourmets) have the luxury of using charcoal for broiling. Many campgrounds provide charcoal stoves. Essentially, charcoal is available in two forms—pressed charcoal briquettes, and natural hardwood charcoal. The briquettes do not burn as hot as pure charcoal. They also should be left glowing until they are coated with ash before food is broiled to eliminate any taste of the oil used in making them. This is especially important if you use a liquid starter or if the briquettes themselves are so-called self-starting.

Natural charcoal can be used for grilling as soon as it is hot. It is not treated with oils before it is bagged. Another plus for natural charcoal—it imparts its own delicate flavor in the smoke. I admit that while we don't use charcoal on trail or river, we charcoal-broil regularly at home and everything is tantalizingly delicious, from mushrooms to fish, corn on the cob, steak, and chicken. We use only, but only, natural hardwood chunks of untreated charcoal. This is the type used by better restaurants. It is available in specialty outing stores and an occasional supermarket. In the distant past, when we went car camping cross-country with our children, we carried natural charcoal and a charcoal grill. Before leaving our camp, we never tossed charcoal ash on the ground if there was no fire ring; we dumped it into a strong plastic garbage bag and toted it out with everything else.

STOVES

A camp stove is an essential ingredient for every successful wilderness trip—afoot or afloat—even for the most determined fire-only campers.

Consider these situations:

Because of dry weather open fires are prohibited.

It is virtually impossible to build a fire when a sudden, violent storm sweeps down upon you.

Without belaboring the obvious, a stove is also what makes cooking possible when enjoying such challenging activities as hiking above timberline and camping in parts of the West and Southwest where the land is barren of wood, or canoeing the Everglades where camping is possible only on platforms erected for tents. (Alligators cannot reach up that high.) Camp stoves also make it convenient to heat quickly a small quantity of food or water without building a fire.

Camp stoves come in two basic formats: the double-burner stove, highly popular with car campers, and the single-burner stove. Both types are available for either liquid or gas fuel.

Single stoves range in size from a self-contained unit not much larger than a fist, which can support the weight of a pot with 3 quarts of water—suitable chiefly for the solo camper, or a couple— to large, sturdy models that can bear the weight of a pot filled with 2 to 2½ gallons of water.

A single camp stove, left, and a double stove. Both attach to separate tanks holding butane or propane as fuel. Good for three-season camping.

The easiest stoves to put into service are those that burn butane or propane. Screw the canister onto the stove unit, flick a match, and it's burning. The drawbacks: Gas fuels don't burn as hot as liquid; they don't function well at temperatures below freezing; and empty gas canisters are heavy but must be toted out with the rest of the garbage.

Most gasoline stoves are designed to burn only white gasoline, although many of the latest models burn either white or leaded gas, alcohol, or kerosene. All are safe to use but can flare up if over-primed, overheated, or carelessly handled. Unleaded gasoline is generally available throughout North America. If you're an international traveler, choose a model that will burn leaded gasoline as well as white, because leaded gas is found worldwide. Stoves with built-in pressure pumps are the easiest to light.

All gasoline stoves require regular cleaning and maintenance. If properly handled a stove can simmer a pot of stew as quickly today as it did when you first tried it out in the backyard 25 years ago.

A small packer's four-season stove, using gasoline in self-contained tank as fuel.

The actual weight of a gasoline stove includes not only the weight of the stove unit itself but also the weight and size of the fuel bottle attached to it when it's beside your tent and you're ready to put a hearty meal together.

Following are descriptions of some popular stoves:

Optimus 111: Weight 54 ounces, including the gas canister built into the stove; the total unit is self-contained in its own metal casing; it burns leaded and unleaded gasoline, and kerosene. A heavy, sturdy stove that is a rough, tough, reliable workhorse of the outdoor fraternity.

Optimus 123: Weight 12 ounces, a self-contained unit; it burns white gasoline. Excellent for small backpacking groups and families.

Optimus 8R: Weight 13 ounces, white gasoline, self-contained. One of the smallest gasoline stoves on the market and useful when size is a critical factor.

Heat collar, used to encircle a small mountain stove to keep wind from blowing away heat. A couple of pot lids can also be used as a heat shield.

Camping Gaz Turbo 270 HP: Weight about 10 ounces without canister; butane-propane mixture; simple to use; not recommended for winter or cold-weather camping.

Peak 1, unleaded 442: Weight about 24 ounces; leaded and white gas. A popular family unit. The new stove performs better in cold weather than the original.

Coleman two-burner: Weight about 9 ounces without canister; propane. Best for casual family and car campers. Not recommended in cold weather.

MSR Rapid Fire: Weight about 12 ounces without canister; iso or butane; well liked by backpackers. Not recommended for cold weather.

MSR Whisperlite: Weight about 14 ounces without canister; white gas; carried by high mountaineers.

MSR X/GK: Weight about 1 pound without canister; will burn white, leaded, or unleaded gas, kerosene, diesel fuel, and Stoddard Solvent No. 1. It's hard to even imagine you can't find a fuel to use in this model no matter how remote the region where your travels take you.

- Take into account when buying a stove that you cannot look inside a propane or butane canister to see how much fuel is inside. When the flame stops, then you know. All liquid fuel stove tanks should be filled before you start to cook.

  Stoves should never be used inside a closed tent. The danger is possible asphyxiation.

- When two stoves are important, I recommend two individual stoves rather than a double-burner model. The great advantage of individual stoves is that they can be set up independently of each other, a noticeable pleasure when cooking simultaneously involves two large pots that tend to nudge each other off the centers of the burners of a double stove, or when two cooks are at work at the same elbow-to-elbow moment.

- On my group trips, whether two-day canoe adventures on local rivers or weeklong backpacking journeys somewhere on the Appalachian Trail, we carry two Optimus 111s. At almost every dinner we light up at least one: The grill is fully occupied broiling appetizing teriyaki chicken, or baby back ribs, or pungent grilled Cajun canned ham, and a hearty soup needs to be cooked simultaneously for a luscious meal.

OPERATING STOVES

After you purchase a camp stove, make sure you try it out at home before you head for camp. If it doesn't work the way you believe it should, now is the time to call the store and clear up any little mysteries about its operation.

If you have a camp stove that you have used before, check that one at home, too, before loading up for the family outing. Make certain it is in full operating condition. I once watched a camper light his stove and complain that it wasn't nearly as hot or efficient as it seemed to be when he first used it. The reason: He had never cleaned the unit of carbon deposits per the instructions that came with it.

When you're filling a gasoline stove, leave a little space at the top of the fuel tank so pressure can be properly built up there when you light the stove.

Even a light breeze can affect the efficiency of a stove in camp. This loss of heat can be reduced by placing some type of windscreen around the tent. We often use a pot lid or a small sheet of aluminum foil placed on the windward side of the stove to deflect the breeze. Under no circumstances should you place a self-designed windscreen around the stove that completely shuts off any breeze. If it's too tight it could reflect enough heat to cause the stove to explode.

If your stove uses a pump to build up pressure for lighting, oil the valve from time to time. Use only pure oil.

There's a much easier way to fill a fuel tank than trying to pour gasoline directly from the can into the tiny tank opening. Carry a small funnel with the stove. If the tank runs dry in the middle of cooking, always wait until the stove cools before pouring in fuel.

And it bears repeating that going inside a tent to cook when the weather turns violent is not recommended. Carbon monoxide is a poison.

BOIL THAT WATER, KILL THAT *GIARDIA—*?

In one quick answer: How do you make water safe to drink when you travel in the wilderness?

Even a 10-year-old knows two methods: Pump it through a water filter. Boil it.

But if you boil it, you may ask, for how long? Five minutes? Ten minutes? Is it the same length of time at sea level as at 8,000 feet?

The correct answer: It is only necessary to heat water to a temperature of 122 degrees F, or 50 C. This, according to William W. Forgey E.D., a trustee of the Wilderness Education Association, Fellow of the Explorer's Club, author of such highly respected books as *Wilderness Medicine, Hypothermia,* and *Essentials of Outdoor First*

The PUR waterfilter, Hiker's model, weighs about 11 ounces. It can pump a fast two pints a minute. Although the filter can pump water directly from a stream, if the water is muddy it's a smart idea to carry a pail of water to camp, let the muck settle, then pump the water from the pail to a clean container.

Aid, and specialist on subzero medicine, is one method of making certain your water is safe to drink.

Dr. Forgey says that just bringing water to this temperature "is adequate to kill all pathogenic organisms," the ugly bugs that affect our digestive system.

However, since few campers carry a cooking thermometer, you should boil your water. Then you'll know it has reached the minimum temperature.

Microfiltration with water filters can be highly effective but, the doctor warned, "it does have its limits.

"Among the most harmful organisms which we actually encounter in natural water supplies are the viral pathogens. Microfiltration cannot eliminate polio, rotovirus, etcetera, but the absorption characteristics of these various filters can be of help."

He pointed out that some water filters work by the "adhesion to the surface of the particles to their interiors. The adsorption process is finite, and eventually the filter is loaded and starts passing nonadsorbed substances clear through."

In other words, if you're using a water filter, make certain you keep a reasonable record of how many gallons have been pumped through it, and either change or clean the filter, depending upon which system you are using, after pumping the recommended amount.

There are a couple of obvious advantages to water-filtering systems. One is that they work immediately. In other words, you don't have to build a fire, put the water on to heat, and wait. Pump and drink.

The other: A filter that can be carried in a backpack can also go into a suitcase. Which means that when you are traveling, especially in third-world countries where the local water could be a problem, you have your own private water purification system with you.

Dr. Forgey noted that both chlorine and iodine are highly effective for treating water. He said that it is safe to use "the recommended concentration of either agent for proper water treatment—even for extended periods of time," for both men and women.

THE *GIARDIA* ARE COMING

Undoubtedly, the reason most wilderness travelers either boil water or use effective filters is to protect themselves against *giardiasis*. However, Dr. James A. Wilkerson, author of *Medicine for Mountaineering*, has said scientific research has shown that the disease is "not the scourge it has been regarded." He explained that in one experiment in which a group of people was given water to drink that had been deliberately heavily contaminated with *Giardia*, "only half" developed an infestation. Of those, "only about a fourth felt any symptoms which, even if totally untreated, disappeared in about 7 to 10 days." It takes about seven days for giardiasis to develop.

It is wise for all campers to have in their first-aid kit an effective medication to treat major dysentery.

In 1995, the *Journal on Wilderness and Environmental Medicine* reported the results of a national survey of state health departments concerning giardiasis cases. It found that only two were traced to backpackers. The authors of the survey reported: "Neither health department surveillance nor the medical literature support the widely held perception that Giardiasis is a significant risk to backpackers in the United States."

Now, read the next sentences with care:

> Giardiasis and similar enteric illness in developed nations ARE OVERWHELMINGLY SPREAD BY DIRECT FECAL/ORAL OR FOOD-BORNE TRANSMISSION, not by contaminated drinking water. Given the casual approach to personal hygiene that characterizes most backpackers, handwashing is likely to be a much more useful preventive strategy than water disinfection.

In a report on research into *Giardia,* Dr. Gordon Benner, medical adviser to the Sierra Club Outing Committee, wrote in *Inside Outings,* a publication for Sierra Club trip leaders, in part:

> It's time to stop worrying about giardia. I admit I do carry a little backup iodine in case my only water source is just downstream from a heavily used campsite. Potable aqua pills are cheap and light, and you can disguise the taste with the powder of your choice, (e.g. lemonade, vitamin C, gatorade). But I do love fresh mountain water, and I drink a lot of it, untreated.

(As a matter of fact, so do I.)

On one of our trips, a pleasant paddler with a soft smile and unruly hair who had brought his own filter talked with me about his reason for filtering water rather than drinking what we boiled in camp.

What was he concerned with?

Dysentery, he said.

I asked how many gallons could be pumped through his filter for purification.

The instructions said it was good for up to 100 gallons.

And, I asked, how many gallons had he pumped through it? Reluctantly, he admitted that he had no idea. How contaminated was the water? No idea. Had he ever changed his filter? Ah, not on several trips, but he intended to.

On another weeklong Sierra trip, two of our guests were a couple in their late 60s. They had been active outdoorspeople for more than 30 years, roaming the wilderness of Asia and both North and South America.

He said that since he and his wife had begun carrying their own water filters instead of using iodine or water-purification tablets, they had not had a single case of diarrhea. They made a note of each time they used the purifier, and carried an extra filter with them.

CAMP WATER

Camping good sense dictates that you draw your water from the cleanest place possible. Water next to the shore is where pollution is most likely to be found. When canoeing, our water detail paddles well out from the shore to fill containers. Backpackers should wade as far from shore as possible to fill their water buckets.

A significant indication of contaminated water is evidence of animals. Whether you heat water or use a water filter, go upstream from a beaver lodge or any sign of animal droppings to draw water. A bubbling spring is usually a fine sign of no animal contamination.

It also is an obligation for those who enjoy the wilderness not to contaminate the water, even as it is for factories not to dump contaminants into our rivers, and communities to treat sewage properly.

Here are some ways all family campers can protect the cleanliness of our streams and lakes:

- Dump dirty kitchen water in a hole 100 feet from the nearest fresh water. Cover with ground detritus when breaking camp.
- When taking a bath, wash and rinse yourself on the shore.

- When washing clothes, use the same procedure.
- Use only soap, which is biodegradable, for all personal and camp use—never detergents.
- It bears repeating: Go at least 200 feet from any water source before digging your private or family cat hole. Wash your hands when you are through.
- Even deep water is not an acceptable dumping ground for empty bottles, cans, or plastic containers. They go out with you in your garbage bag.

Keeping wilderness water clean is everyone's responsibility.

DINING WELL

For some, family cooking in camp from fresh ingredients is a joy. For others, freeze-dried meals that can be prepared in a few moments are the only way to enjoy the wilderness. Fortunately, this is one thing families who hike, canoe, bike, travel via pack train, or car camp can have both ways. Even the wilderness gourmets, to whom an outstanding meal never came in an add-hot-water package, will, on occasion, choose and enjoy freeze-dried meals or dishes. And lightweight travelers will, when their palates grow weary of heat-and-eat dishes, freshen their taste buds with a genuine camp-cooked dish.

Naturally, the gourmet chef uses only the freshest fruits, vegetables, and meats at home. But then it's easy to switch to canned, freeze-dried, and dehydrated meats for camping, as well as small cans of seafoods, chicken, and meat. These foods are widely available in supermarkets, outing stores, health food stores, ethnic grocery stores, and companies that specialize in epicurean meals when the only refrigerator is the shade of a tree with the food bags stashed against it.

What foods you choose to take will depend both on what's popular at home, especially with children, and in some measure on the type of outing you will be going on. If, by way of an example, you plan to spend a three-day weekend on a canoe trip, or carry

Whether it's a soup of fresh ingredients or delicious snacks sitting on the camp table, almost every food the family dines on at home can be prepared on a long weekend camp.

food to a base camp by car, you can take all the foods your family enjoys at home with you. Here is how to keep them reasonably fresh: Freeze everything that won't be affected by the cold, such as candy, nuts, bread, pasta, rice, margarine, meat, and chicken. Chill the fresh eggs, vegetables, and fruits. Put all the food in an ice chest, add a frozen container or two of "ice" solution, and you are set for three days.

Even if the family will be backpacking or bike camping, freeze-dried and dehydrated meals, vegetables, and soups can be balanced by some of the fresh vegetables and fruits the children enjoy at home, as well as fresh meat or poultry for the first day or two.

READ THE LABEL

Whether you shop at a supermarket or an outing goods store, when your menu includes any precooked dishes or meals, powdered soups, or quick-cooking carbohydrates, it is critical to read the label on each package to see how many it will serve. A soup container that says it will serve three—but each serving is only 6 ounces—certainly is not going to be enough to feed two hungry adults plus even one hearty young appetite. All of you can easily consume 10 to 12 ounces apiece at dinner.

A family will eat 10 to 20 percent more after even a casual day in the outdoors than at the dining room table after a vigorous day of playing the Internet or staring at a wild, chilling killer-gets-his TV program.

On an active outing a reasonable estimate of daily caloric needs is 3,500 per adult—more for men, less for women. Teenagers can easily wolf down 4,000 to 4,500 calories per day; for an all-adult-male trip, figure about 4,000 calories per person.

Take out the confusion that inevitably arises in camp when meals and menus are based upon the "I guess we ought to have some of this, and maybe toss in some of that" system. Instead, plan in advance.

Each meal.

Each dish.

Each condiment.

Then make out a detailed shopping chart that includes every item. Including the powdered milk for each day.

You'll keep a more accurate record of your purchases if you don't put anything into the food bags or food utility bag until all your shopping is complete. Mark on the outside of each bag what day it is for (day 1, day 2, day 3, and so on), then line up the bags, the food that goes into each, and pack. Remember to put the appropriate amount of dried milk into each day's bag.

All the spices and condiments, sugar, coffee, salt, pepper, hot chocolate, tea, margarine, mayonnaise, mustard and catsup in plastic bottles, et al., for the entire trip go into the food utility bag.

Pack the food utility bag last.

QUANTITIES

An excellent way to figure food quantities is to use the chart on recommended amounts per person from the Sierra Club totebook *Food for Knapsackers and Other Trail Travelers* by Hasse Bunnelle, reprinted on pages 86–89.

Although Bunnelle did not include them on his condiment list, every well-stocked supply should also include plastic bottles of lemon juice, balsamic and cider vinegar, and, if you're not already carrying it, some wine. Here is how these ingredients add that delicious extra touch to the flavor of foods by balancing the taste.

As professional cooks know, all foods should have a balance of salty and sweet, bitter and acidic, yet the addition of an acid, or another touch of salt, is often neglected. As one example, we were having chili one evening when the cook, after a couple of tastings, said: "Something's missing."

A couple of eager, hungry volunteer tasters agreed.

As it turned out, the chili got a surprisingly tasty uplift from a light sprinkling of more salt and a tablespoon of balsamic vinegar.

For those who must reduce salt on the personal advice of their physician—not on the recommendation of the coolest batch of with-it health writers—try what the expert chefs at the Tante Marie Cooking School in San Francisco recommend to improve the flavor of food: Soy sauce as a salt replacement, and Tabasco sauce instead of additional pepper.

The Allison restaurant, in New York, recommends a "spritz" of lemon juice to add flavor to sautèed or steamed vegetable dishes, and vinegar to enhance the taste of stews.

When packing food bags for the out-of-doors eliminate bulk and garbage by getting rid of all boxes and repackaging the food, if necessary, in plastic bags. Unless you really want confusion, remember to tear off the directions and pop them into the appropriate plastic bags. The bags can be taken home and reused.

Never carry anything in glass jars or bottles. Liquids and powders can be put into plastic bottles. Use widemouthed bottles into which you can put a tablespoon.

TRAIL SNACKS

A light snack to nibble on to ease those hunger pains when the next meal is still miles in the distance is a subject of special interest to active youngsters and, equally often, to their parents. Some campers hand everyone a commercial "golly, this-is-a-full-of-wonderful-special-healthful-energy" bar after breakfast. Or, you may prefer to fabricate your own snack pack out of GORP. The name GORP is believed to be an acronym for "Good Old Raisins and Peanuts," first mixed together 100 years ago for New England trailhikers to snack on. Make yours according to your own taste of both tasty and nutritious items, such as mixed nuts, raisins, M&Ms, minced dried fruits, toasted soybeans, sesame twigs, sunflower seeds, and whatever else you and the children munch on with pleasure.

A plastic bag filled with a couple of ounces distributed to everyone every morning will give eager young hands something to pop into an open mouth at any time during the day. Warning: Do not take leftover GORP into a tent at night. Big and little animals alike find it delicious.

Food	Ounces per person per day	Calories	Comments
BREAKFAST			
Dried fruits	1.5	110	Excellent when eaten dry, mixed with cereal or simmered.
Cereals; compact cold cereals such as various granolas, Familia, Grape Nuts, etc.	1.5	150–180	Avoid presugared cereals, or cereals with high sugar content. Sugars add bulk without adding nutritional value.
Instant hot cereals: Quaker Oats, Wheatena, Cream of Wheat, etc.	1.5	150	Some are prepared by simply adding hot water, others must be boiled for a minute or two. Cereals with such extras as raisins, fruits, or flavorings are especially popular. If the cereal does not contain any, add them yourself. (Note: Cereals commercially packaged into individual servings usually contain portions too small for husky camp appetites. Figure on one and one-half packages per person.)
Bacon, Spam	1.4	250–300	For long trips buy the canned varieties. Use the grease for cooking.
Boneless ham or shoulder	1.4	160	Take precooked only.
Eggs	two per person	170	Whether fresh, freeze-dried, or dehydrated, eggs are a breakfast staple.
Potatoes, dehydrated and prepackaged	1.0	150–200	Available in supermarkets; exceptionally popular.
Pancake mixes	2.0	200	Popular, but drags out a breakfast. Reserve for days when you'll be in camp.
LUNCH			
Crackers, such as RyKrisp	1.5	175	Keep well and are excellent with peanut butter and jelly.
Firm "German" or Westphalian pumpernickel	1.5	100	Also keeps well, but is more likely to be crushed than firm crackers.
Various dry salamis and bolognas	1.5	120–150	Many varieties keep well without refrigeration.
Cheeses	1.5	170	Look for hard cheeses (such as Monterey jack, Swiss, or provolone) or those canned cheeses that do not need refrigeration. On shorter trips try the canned French cheeses such as Brie and Camembert. Avoid cheeses with unusual and strong flavors.
Tuna fish, salmon, sardines	1.5	125	Canned tuna can be served as is, or mixed with mayonnaise or sandwich spread.

Food	Ounces per person per day	Calories	Comments
L U N C H (CONT.)			
Deviled meats	1.5	Varies	Sample at home; some types are quite spicy.
Gorp	1.0	220	Use salted nuts or salted soybeans when mixing gorp, especially in hot weather.
Nuts, various	1.0	1.75	
Peanut butter	1.0	200	A luncheon favorite.
Jelly	0.3	80	To add a touch of something special to the peanut butter.
Candy	0.5	75	Avoid candy that melts.
Dried fruits	1.3	100	Raisins and apples are the most popular.
Powdered drink mixes, including instant ice coffee and tea		Varies	The label will give you the approximate amount per cupful.
D I N N E R			
Soup, dehydrated	Varies	Check on label.	Packaged soups specify the servings in either 6- or 8-ounce amounts. Figure on 12 liquid ounces per person.
Sauces and gravy mixes	Varies	Check on label.	Usually a package makes an 8-ounce cupful. Popular with almost every starch dish from mashed potatoes to couscous.
Meat, fresh—steak, boneless	5.0	250	A fine main course the first night in camp.
Fowl, fresh—chicken, turkey	16.0	140	Chickens broil in about 40 minutes; turkey takes much longer. Also best the first night at your put-in.
Canned corned beef			
Canned roast beef	3.0	200	
Canned ham, boneless	3.0	230	For large groups, buy the meat in No. 10 cans. Quantities and servings are usually clearly specified and accurate.
Canned chicken, turkey	3.0	220	
Canned tuna	3.0	250	
Freeze-dried beef, chops, patties	1.0	130	
Pasta, noodles	3.0	300	
Precooked rice	2.0	200	

Food	Ounces per person per day	Calories	Comments
DINNER (CONT.)			
Dehydrated mashed potatoes	1.6	160	
Dehydrated potato dishes, such as au gratin or scalloped		210	Servings specified on the label are about 50% less than hungry adults will eat in camp.
Couscous, kasha		160	Serve with a light gravy mix.
Desserts: Jell-O, instant pudding, instant cheesecake, etc.			
STAPLES			
Coffee, instant	0.15	0	
Tea, instant		0	
Tea bags	2 bags	0	
Hot chocolate mix	1.0	150	
Nonfat dry milk			
Flour or biscuit mix		100	Buy in prepackaged 1-quart envelopes; figure on 1½ quarts per day per four people. The box will indicate the number of biscuits its contents will make; judge accordingly. Mixes also can be used for thickening instead of ordinary flour.
Sugar	1.0	100	An artificial sweetener will substantially reduce the amount of sugar bulk you must carry.
Dehydrated soup greens	0.1		For enriching many dishes.
Dehydrated onion flakes	0.1		For enriching many dishes.
Dried mushrooms	0.15		
Buy dried Chinese mushrooms.	1.0		
Margarine	230	230	Read the label; some require no refrigeration and will keep for several weeks.

CONDIMENTS*

Salt
Pepper
Basil
Thyme
Oregano
Chili powder
Curry powder
Ginger, powdered
Tarragon
Cloves
Red pepper
Sesame seed
Chervil
Parsley
Bouillon cubes
Garlic or garlic powder
Rosemary
Cumin
Marjoram
Cinnamon
Maple flavoring   Useful if you make your own syrup out of sugar.

*Plus any others your recipes call for.

MENUS AND RECIPES

Our wilderness meals include popular food, but we also try to add an unusual dish here and there to make any meal a bit more interesting. Except for dinner, we tend to keep meals simple, tasty, and quick to prepare.

When planning your shopping, figure quantities based upon what your family eats, or, if in doubt, follow Bunnelle's recommendations.

BREAKFAST

Following are some menus and recipes we enjoy for breakfasts. For hot cereal, we use small packets of various instant cereals, one and one-half packages per adult. Cold cereal is whatever you choose, but the "compact" cereals, not the toasted flakes, are a better choice if you'll be carrying yours in a backpack.

Your drink can be whatever pleases the family, such as milk made from powdered mix, hot chocolate, tea, brewed or instant coffee, and powdered drinks.

Fruit compote is made by chopping up dried fruit, covering it generously with water, and simmering for about 10 minutes. Use it instead of hot water or hot milk on instant cereal. Usually about ¼ cup of chopped fruits will serve a family of four. Make more or less, as you desire.

Day 1: Huevos Gordonos, hot cereal, fruit compote, drink.

H U E V O S   G O R D O N O S

Bacon, 2 slices per tortilla

Freeze-dried, dehydrated, or fresh eggs, 2 per adult (freeze-dried are much tastier than dehydrated)

Tortillas, 2 per adult

Salsa

1. Fry bacon very crisp.
2. Make a single pot of scrambled eggs.
3. Heat tortillas about 30 seconds, just to warm.
4. Put a serving of scrambled eggs on a tortilla.
5. Add some crisp bacon.
6. Top with a little salsa.
7. Roll up tortilla and serve.

F R U I T   C O M P O T E

¼ mixed dried fruits

1. Chop up dried fruits and cover generously with water. Simmer for 10 minutes.

Day 2: Potato pancakes (follow package directions), applesauce, cold cereal, drink. Remember to make milk.

Day 3: Fried rice, hot cereal with fruit compote, drink. The fried rice is an excellent way to use leftover rice from last night. Or simply cook 2 extra cups of rice for dinner and save them for breakfast.

Cooking oil

1 small onion, minced

2 celery stalks, with leaves, sliced into ¼-inch pieces

2 quarter-size slices peeled, minced fresh ginger

2 cups cold rice

4 eggs, fresh or freeze-dried

2 tablespoons soy sauce

1. In large frying pan or pot, heat 2 tablespoons oil, add onion and celery, and sauté over low heat for five minutes.
2. Add minced ginger and sauté two minutes.
3. Add rice; stir thoroughly until hot. Push to one side of pan.
4. Whip eggs in small bowl, then pour into other side of pan. Stir while cooking. Slowly mix the cooking eggs with the rice. Stir-fry until eggs are cooked.
5. Add soy sauce. Give final mix. Serve.

Day 4: Hotcakes, cold cereal, drink.

HOTCAKES

Hotcake mix (Recommended: Mix that already includes powdered milk so you need add only water before cooking)

1. If frying pan is small, make "dollar" size; serve with usual choice of syrup.

Day 5: Corned beef hash, hot cereal, fruit compote, drink.

CORNED BEEF HASH

1-pound can corned beef hash

1. Set an open can in a pot of hot water to heat, or heat the hash in a frying pan.

Day 6: Oeufs aux fine herbes, bacon (½ pound), cold cereal, drink.

OEUFS

2 eggs per person

Herbes de Provence

1. Make a single pot of scrambled eggs.
2. Add 1 teaspoon Herbes de Provence per six eggs.

LUNCHES

In camp or for the traveling family, lunches tend to follow the same pattern: salamis, canned fish, cheeses, firm bread or crackers, powdered drinks, and something pleasant such as hard candies or dried fruits. The exception is adding a hot, quick-cooking food on a cold day. Here are the ingredients we usually make our lunch selections from:

Canned fish: These include canned tuna and salmon, as well as an occasional can of mackerel, sardines, or, rarely, shrimp, mussels, clams, or oysters. The fish is put into a dish and served with tartar sauce or mayonnaise, although mustard and catsup may pop up from time to time. The particular fish sauce is no accident, but planned in advance at home.

Meats: The meat of choice is some type of salami or deviled meat, although we occasionally add canned chicken or Spam. The salamis and bolognas are always served cut into slices, with a sauce such as mustard or catsup on the side.

Cheeses: The range is wonderfully broad. Recommended: Only genuine cheese, not cheese substitutes. Carry soft cheeses in plastic containers so they won't end up squished to mush in a pack. We always serve them cut into serving portions.

Peanut butter in a plastic bottle and jelly in a squeeze bottle: This combination is served with every lunch.

Breads: Large crackers, such as RyKrisp, or firm breads, such as Westphalian rye.

Specials: How about cornichon gherkins, or sun-dried tomatoes, or pickles?

Fruit: On backpacking trips we take only small fresh fruits, such as tangerines or small apples, that will keep well for several hot summer days. Otherwise, dried fruits.

Candy: Something hard or chewy as a bit of lunch dessert.

Drink: Cold mix-yourself drink powders.

Cold-weather foods: If you face the prospect of cold weather, pick out
some foods that can be served by either heating or adding hot
water, such as boxed macaroni and cheese, or the new noodle
soups in cup-size containers. Keep them as replacements for the
planned luncheon menu.

Here are two typical lunch menus:

Menu 1 : Canned salmon with tartar sauce, Brie cut into serving
wedges, peanut butter and jelly, firm crackers, hard candy, dried
apricots, drink.

Menu 2: Salami and kielbasa slices served with mustard and catsup,
Camembert cut into wedges, sun-dried tomatoes, Westphalian
rye, peanut butter and jelly with raisins to sprinkle on the peanut
butter, tangerines (take the peelings out with you), hard candy,
drink.

Hungry? It's time for lunch. Make your own sandwich.

DINNER

Dinners are another matter. They are social events, not just the
gulping down of a meal. Ours feature some dishes that are rather
complicated to prepare. It's fine with us: We have the time for
longer preparation and more abundant eating. Those who prepare
add-hot-water foods because cooking takes up extra time spend the
evenings after dinner doing what other diners do. Sitting around.
Talking. And waiting until it's time to turn in.

Our dinners are basically three-course meals: soup, main course,
and a carbohydrate food such as potatoes or couscous. Sometimes we
add an advance plate of crudités; always, a dessert.

We begin every dinner with soup. This is because people active
in the outdoors usually become slightly dehydrated during the day
and soup is a tasty way to help the body restore fluid balance.

SOUPS

Following are some recipes for superior camp soups, four to five portions apiece.

BLACK BEAN SOUP

1 1-pound can black beans, rinsed and drained

2 tablespoons dried onion flakes

1 teaspoon minced garlic

2½ cups water

1 8-ounce can tomatoes, chopped but not drained

1 jalapeño pepper, minced (very spicy)

1 teaspoon ground cumin

1 teaspoon oregano

1 bay leaf

Salt and pepper to taste

1. In large pot mix all ingredients. Bring to a boil and simmer 10 minutes. Add more water if necessary.

GREEK LENTIL SOUP

½ pound lentils

2 tablespoons onion flakes

2 garlic cloves, minced

1 1-pound can whole tomatoes, chopped but not drained

5 chicken bouillon cubes dissolved in 5 cups water

1 teaspoon dried parsley

3 teaspoons mint leaves

1 bay leaf

2 tablespoons olive oil

1 tablespoon vinegar

1. In large pot, add lentils, onion, garlic, tomatoes, and bouillon, bring to a boil, cover, and simmer 30 minutes.
2. Add parsley, mint, bay leaf, and oil and simmer another 10 minutes or until lentils are tender.
3. Add vinegar. Remove from heat. Stir and let stand five minutes. Remove bay leaf before serving.

CAMBODIAN SOUP

2 cloves garlic, minced

1 small jalapeño pepper, sliced into a few thin rings (warning: very hot)

1 tablespoon margarine

8 ounces canned chicken

2 tablespoons onion flakes

5 cups water

2 tablespoons lemon juice

3 inches lemongrass, fresh or dried

½ teaspoon basil

Salt and pepper to taste

1. In large pot sauté garlic and jalapeño slices in 1 tablespoon margarine for three minutes. Do not brown garlic.
2. Add chicken, onion flakes, and water, bring to a boil, lower heat, and simmer five minutes. Add lemon juice and lemongrass and simmer another three minutes, stirring constantly.
3. Sprinkle with basil before serving.

SHIITAKE CHICKEN SOUP

Four large dried shiitake mushrooms

Packaged chicken noodle soup for 6

2 quarter-size slices peeled fresh ginger

2 tablespoons soy sauce

1 tablespoon onion flakes

1. Soak mushrooms 30 minutes in hot water only to cover. Do not drain. (If using fresh mushrooms, do not soak.) Trim stems. Slice tops.
2. Follow directions for soup, except add reserved mushroom water.
3. Add mushroom caps and all other ingredients to soup. Simmer five minutes longer than packaged soup directions call for.

QUICK TOMATO SOUP

Packages of tomato soup to serve 6

1 6-ounce can tomato juice

1 tablespoon dried basil

1. Place soup mix in a pot. Add water plus tomato juice to equal the amount called for on the package directions. Add basil.

2. Simmer per directions and serve.

MATZO BALL (DUMPLING) SOUP

> Packaged matzo ball mix
>
> Packaged chicken soup without noodles to serve 6, or substitute 6 cups chicken bouillon
>
> 1 tablespoon onion flakes

1. Prepare matzo balls per directions.
2. Make chicken soup per directions in separate pot of water. Add onion flakes.
3. When matzo dumplings are ready, add to soup.

CHICKEN ORZO SOUP

> 6 bouillon cubes dissolved in 6 cups water
>
> 1 4-ounce can chicken
>
> ½ cup orzo
>
> 2 eggs, fresh or reconstituted
>
> 2 tablespoons lemon juice

1. Bring bouillon to a boil, add chicken and orzo, cover, and simmer 10 minutes.
2. In separate bowl mix eggs and lemon juice. Slowly pour in 1 cup of the hot soup, stirring constantly.
3. Pour mixture slowly back into soup, stir, add more water if necessary, and serve.

MAIN DISHES

So, what's for dinner? Try some of these recipes on your next outing. All are for four to five people.

LENTILS CÔTE D'AZUR

> 2 tablespoons margarine
>
> ½ cup onion flakes presoaked 10 minutes in enough water to cover, and drained
>
> 1 clove garlic, minced
>
> 6 bouillon cubes dissolved in 6 cups water
>
> ½ pound lentils
>
> 1 bay leaf

1 teaspoon thyme

1 6-ounce can tomato paste

½ pound favorite salami, cut into thin slices

1. In large pot, melt margarine and sauté onion and garlic for three minutes. Do not brown garlic.
2. Add bouillon, lentils, bay leaf, and thyme, and simmer 20 minutes.
3. Add tomato paste and continue simmering another 10 minutes or until lentils are tender. Stir in salami slices. Add more water if necessary.

CORNED BEEF RODRIGUEZ

1 pound canned corned beef

3 tablespoons onion flakes, presoaked 10 minutes in enough water to cover; do not drain

3 garlic cloves, minced

3 ounces tomato paste

1 small can black olives, drained and chopped

½ teaspoon oregano

½ teaspoon Herbes de Provence

1. Add all ingredients to pot. Add enough water to moisten thoroughly. Heat to a simmer for 10 minutes, stirring frequently.

CURRIED TURKEY WITH SAMBALS

¼ cup margarine

2 tablespoons flour

2 tablespoons curry powder

1 teaspoon turmeric

1 teaspoon coriander

2 cups milk

1 pound canned turkey

Sambals

Chutney

1. In large pot melt margarine, then slowly stir in flour, curry powder, turmeric, and coriander over low heat until it makes a smooth paste. Add milk slowly until paste becomes a sauce. Crumble turkey chunks into sauce.
2. For Sambals, fill cups with various nuts, chopped dried fruits, banana flakes, raisins, or whatever else interests your hungry

consumers. Diners cover their turkey with the sambals they want, and top with chutney.

TAHITI CHILI

¼ cup onion flakes, presoaked 10 minutes barely covered with water; do not drain

2 cloves garlic, minced

1 4-ounce can green chilies

1 tablespoon margarine

1 pound canned corned beef, or canned beef

1 tablespoon cumin seed

1 pound canned tomatoes

4 ounces tomato paste

2 tablespoons mild chili powder

1. In large pot combine onions, garlic, and chilies in 1 tablespoon margarine and stir-fry for three minutes.
2. Add crumbled corned beef or chopped-up beef, cumin seed, tomatoes with juice, tomato paste, and chili powder with enough water to bring chili to desired thickness. Simmer for 10 minutes. Serve with chili powder on the side for those who like more spice.

SPAGHETTI WITH CRAB SAUCE

8 ounces canned crab, picked over to remove any shell

4 tablespoons olive oil, divided

3 garlic cloves, minced

2 tablespoons onion flakes soaked in enough water to cover for 10 minutes

Cayenne pepper to taste (be gentle)

1 8-ounce can tomatoes, chopped, with juice

½ cup red wine

1 tablespoon oregano

1 tablespoon basil

1 tablespoon Herbes de Provence

3 ounces tomato paste

1 pound spaghetti

1. For the crab sauce, add to a large pot the crab meat and 2 tablespoons of the oil, stir-fry over low heat for one minute. Add garlic,

onion, and cayenne pepper and continue stir-frying for another minute.

2. Add tomatoes with juices and stir-fry another minute.
3. Add wine, spices, and tomato paste and stir-fry another couple of minutes. If the sauce is too thick, add water.
4. Bring a separate large pot of water to boil, add the remaining oil and the spaghetti, and cook for about 10 minutes, or until al dente. Drain and serve with hot crab sauce.

TERIYAKI HAM

½ cup teriyaki sauce

2 tablespoons soy sauce

1 tablespoon sugar

1 pound canned ham

Canned wasabi powder

1. Mix teriyaki sauce, soy sauce and sugar in small pot. Heat only until sugar is dissolved.
2. Cut ham into slices. Place slices in a Ziploc bag and pour in sauce. Squeeze air out of bag, zip shut, let ham marinate at least a half hour.
3. Broil ham over hot coals, not flames, for 10 minutes, brushing occasionally with sauce. Serve with wasabi sauce, made per instructions on can. Wasabi is very spicy; make only a small amount.

THE LIGHTWEIGHTS

Backpackers, for whatever reasons, seem to feel that traveling light is not sufficient. They should go ultralight. And this applies to the foods they carry as well. The following recipes for the light-lights are from June Fleming's book *The Well-Fed Backpacker*. It is especially interesting for those who would like to prepare and package lightweight dishes at home.

BOUILLABAISSE

1 package Knorr bouillabaisse mix

1 4½-ounce can shrimp

1 6½-ounce can clams

1 4½-ounce can smoked mussels

1. Heat 4 cups of water; stir in bouillabaisse mix.

2. Add shrimp, clams, and mussels, with their liquid. Simmer briefly and serve.

SHRIMP CREOLE

½ cup dried tomato bits

¼ cup dried green pepper flakes

1 cup quick rice

1 package cream of mushroom soup mix

1 4½-ounce can shrimp

Salt and pepper to taste

1. Simmer tomato and green pepper with rice for six minutes.
2. Add soup mix and undrained shrimp. Blend thoroughly. Add more hot water if needed.

RICE WITH MEATBALLS

1 cup dried tomato pieces

2 tablespoons dried chopped onion

4 servings freeze-dried or canned meatballs

1 packet brown—or personal favorite—gravy mix

Salt and pepper to taste

1 cup quick rice

1. Cook all ingredients except rice for five minutes in 3-1/2 cups water.
2. Add rice. Cover and cook another eight minutes. Add more water if necessary. Serve.

MULLIGATAWNY

2 cups quick rice

4 servings (read the label) mulligatawny soup mix

¼ cup powdered milk

1 tablespoon margarine

¼ cup sherry (carry it in a plastic bottle)

1 big, fat, juicy red unpared apple, cut into small chunks

Salt and pepper to taste

1. Make rice per package directions.
2. Blend soup mix and milk in 2 cups cold water. Add margarine and simmer for two minutes while stirring.

3. Add sherry to mix, stir, pour over cooked rice, and season. Top
   with apple bits.

CARBOHYDRATES

So far I've talked about breakfasts, lunches, soups, and main dishes. Here are some fast-cooking carbohydrate recipes to fill out a balanced dinner meal.

Quick-cooking rice: This takes 5 to 10 minutes to prepare following the directions on the package.

Potatoes: The dehydrated mashed potatoes found in every store are excellent. They come in various combinations. However, try adding four garlic cloves, boiled for 15 minutes, then crushed and added to four servings of mashed potatoes. Potatoes are also available in a variety of precooked recipes—just add hot water— freeze-dried, and dehydrated.

Couscous: In a large pot heat 2 cups of chicken bouillon with 2 table-spoons of dried onion. Let simmer five minutes. Pour in 1 cup of couscous, stir occasionally for five minutes, and serve. Do not let cooked couscous sit around too long before serving; it becomes chewy.

For a nice touch, save some of the camp soup and let diners add a spoonful or two as a gravy on the couscous. Packaged couscous mixes with added ingredients are also widely available.

Instant black beans: Fantastic Foods–brand beans are ready five minutes after you add boiling water. They also can be converted to an enjoyable camp soup in 15 minutes.

Falafel: Basically, a mix of chick- and yellow peas with dehydrated vegetables rolled into small balls. Fry them in an inch of oil for 15 minutes.

The number of different quick-cooking carbohydrate foods available in supermarkets, ethnic groceries, and outing goods stores increase year by year. Prowl the aisles. Shop slowly. And try something new for your next meal—at home. If it's acceptable to the family, add it to your camping menu.

BEFORE COOKING

Here are some points to keep in mind before starting to cook in camp or on the trail:

1. If you're cooking with fire, be sure that the fire is lighted and burning properly, and that there is enough wood on hand for the entire meal.
2. If you're using a gasoline stove, be sure each tank is properly filled with gas, so the flame doesn't sizzle out in the middle of cooking.
3. If you're in doubt about how much fuel remains in a propane or butane stove, be sure that you know precisely where another cartridge is kept.
4. Have everything you need visibly in front of you, especially all the spices and other ingredients hiding in the food utility bag, before you start preparing that gourmet meal.
5. Read each recipe twice.
6. Now, start cooking.

BROILING MEAT AND POULTRY

If you cook over an open fire, know that more fresh fish, meat, and poultry have been spoiled by the fire than by the cook. Your prime necessities are a bed of hot coals—just as when you're cooking on a charcoal grill—and enough small kindling on hand to maintain the heat until you're done cooking.

Everyone's favorite, steak, is usually completely cooked within 10 minutes or less. Fish broiled in a fish grill should also be cooked for a comparatively short period. Chicken, however, must cook for 35 to 45 minutes. Thus, you should have enough small pieces of wood on hand to feed an occasional piece into the fire when the heat gets low.

Maintain a slow, but steady pace feeding the fire. To build it up in quick passion when it begins to collapse will rate a bed of roaring flames. Ergo, the chicken will be burned on the outside, raw on the inside.

Even a bed of hot coals can erupt into flame if grease drips onto it. There is a sim-

> ## Eat Hearty—In Camp
>
> It's fully permissible to eat like the proverbial pig—when you and the spouse and the children are working off calories by the thousands every day in the wilds. But take warning: When you return to civilization, your body takes several days to figure out you are no longer burning up the calories. It will want you to stuff it in at every meal. Resist the temptation.

ple secret to keeping the flames away, whether from grease or a fresh piece of wood—water. Cook with a large pot of water on hand. Sprinkle every flame lightly. The flame will go out, the hot coals stay hot.

GOLDEN OLDIES

Whatever foods your family enjoys are certainly going to be prepared when you go camping. But meals in camp also can be an adventure in new foods and unexpected ways to prepare them.

Here are a few recipes from Horace Kephart's century-old classic *The Book of Camping and Woodcraft,* which demonstrate the old-timers' understanding of how to make fine dishes on a hunting or fishing trip. The kids probably will get as big a kick out of how they're made as how they taste.

Naturally, they will help with the cooking.

> Home cookery is based upon milk, butter, and eggs; nine-tenths of the recipes in a standard cook-book call for one or more of these ingredients. But it often happens to us campers that our "tin cow" has gone dry, our butter was finished long ago, and as for eggs—we have heard of eggs, but for us they do not exist. In such case, no ordinary cook-book is of any use to us.

This is the way Kephart began his chapter on campfire cooking. But to Kephart, ingredients and recipes were only part of wilderness cooking:

Half of cookery is the fire thereof. It is quite impossible to prepare a good meal over a higgledy-piggledy heap of smoking
chunks, or over a fierce blaze, or over a great bed of coals that
will warp cast-iron and melt everything else.

For today's campers who cook over a woodfire, his advice is
still valid.

Here is his recipe for "Army bread—Bannocks":

> 1 quart flour
> 1 teaspoon salt
> 1 tablespoon full sugar
> 2 heaping teaspoonfuls baking powder

As this is made without grease, it is easier to mix than biscuit
dough. Mix the ingredients thoroughly and stir in enough cold
water (about one and a half pints) to make a thick batter that
will pour out level. Mix rapidly with spoon until smooth, and
pour out at once into Dutch oven or bake-pan. Bake about
forty-five minutes, or until no dough adheres to a sliver stuck in
the loaf. Keeps fresh longer than yeast bread and does not dry
up or mold. This is the kind of bread to bake when you are
laying in a three-day's supply. It is more wholesome than biscuit, and is best eaten cold.

Hint: You also can make Army Bread from Bisquick.

A Boy Scout method of "baking" Bannocks that children
always enjoy is to keep the dough thick, then wrap a ribbon of it
around the top of a clean, preheated stick several feet long. Prop the
stick so the dough is over a hot bed of coals. Turn it slowly from
time to time until cooked and the outside lightly browned. Eat by
breaking chunks off the stick.

A tradition among hunters and fishermen for generations was
a fine Brunswick stew, made with freshly shot squirrels appropri-
ately skinned and cleaned. Today's campfire cook can substitute a
tough, old fowl. It will be tender before the stew is finished.

Kephart's recipe:

The ingredients needed, besides several squirrels, are:

1 qt. can tomatoes;

1 pt. " butter beans or limas,

1 pt. " green corn,

6 potatoes, parboiled and sliced,

½ lb. butter,

½ lb. salt pork (fat),

1 teaspoonful black pepper,

½ " Cayenne

1 tablespoonful salt,

2 tablespoonfuls white sugar,

1 onion minced small

Soak the squirrels half an hour in cold salted water. Add the salt to one gallon of fresh water, and boil five minutes. Then put in the onions, beans, corn, pork (cut into fine strips), potatoes, pepper, and squirrels. Cover closely, and stew very slowly two and a half hours, stirring frequently to prevent burning. Add the tomatoes and sugar, and stew an hour longer. Then add the butter, cut into bits the size of a walnut and rolled in flour. Boil ten minutes. Then serve at once.

Note: If you're using fowl, reduce the simmering time to a total of about one and a half hours, or until the chicken is tender.

Among his recipes is one for cooking a fish before an open fire by planking it. The technique is simple:

Split and smooth a slab of sweet hardwood two or three inches thick, two feet long, and somewhat wider than the opened fish. Prop it in front of a bed of coals till it is sizzling hot. Split the fish down the back its entire length, but do not cut clear through the belly. Clean, and wipe it quite dry. When plank is hot, spread fish out like an opened book, tack it, skin side down, to the planks and prop before fire. Baste continuously with a bit of pork on a switch held above it. Reverse ends of plank from time to time. If the flesh is flaky when pierced with a fork, it is done. Sprinkle salt and pepper over the fish, moisten with drippings, and serve on the hot plank. No better dish ever was set before an epicure.

To which, after planking freshly caught fish, I can only add, amen!

KID CHEFS

Eating in camp is fun. The kids are hungry. So are the moms and dads as they cook up a . . . a what? Because younger children may, or may not, do much cooking at home, should they be shooed away from the cooking fire or camp stove when the family is enjoying the out-of-doors?

I say no. Encourage them to do some of the camp cooking. This means more than just having them wash off the potatoes, or put the plates out. If they are genuinely too young to be trusted stirring, slicing, and cooking over the fire, then turn to simple recipes to let them take part in the family food chain.

For those very young kids, here are some recipes adapted from Janet Bruno's and Peggy Dakan's booklet "Cooking in the Classroom." They taste even better when a cooling breeze is blowing off the lake.

PEANUT BUTTER BALLS

> 1 cup peanut butter
> 1 cup honey
> 1½ cups powdered milk

1. Mix peanut butter and honey in a bowl.
2. Add powdered milk and stir until mixture is thick.
3. Roll into little balls. Serve.
4. Clean up and put everything away.

PINEAPPLE FRUIT GARDEN

> 1 can fruit cocktail
> 1 can sliced pineapple
> Toothpicks

1. Put a pineapple ring in the center of each plate.
2. Stick a piece of fruit on one end of a toothpick, then stick the other in the pineapple. Serve and devour.

TOAD-IN-A-HOLE

> 1 slice bread
>
> Margarine
>
> 1 egg

1. Cut a whole in the center of a slice of bread.
2. Butter the bread and brown both sides in a hot frying pan.
3. Remove the pan from the fire and break an egg into the hole.
4. Put the pan back on the fire, cover, and cook until the egg is done. Serve each person a Toad-in-a-Hole as soon as it is cooked.
5. Clean up and put everything away.

OLIVES AND CHEESES

> Stuffed green olives
>
> A small brick of favorite cheese
>
> Toothpicks
>
> Freshly picked green leaves found around the camp

1. Cut each olive in half.
2. Cut the cheese into small pieces about as big as half an olive.
3. Put a half olive on one end of a toothpick, and a piece of cheese on the other.
4. Arrange them on a platter with fresh leaves scattered around the edges to make it look attractive.
5. Clean up and put everything away.

CAMP PUDDING

> Instant chocolate pudding
>
> Tiny marshmallows

1. Make the pudding in a bottle with a screw-on top.
2. Mix thoroughly. Wait until it begins to get firm.
3. Mix in tiny marshmallows.
4. Pour into individual cups. Serve after dinner.
5. Clean up and put everything away.

Menus

If you will be camping in remote areas where buying fresh groceries is difficult—or impossible—then you must bring everything you'll cook in camp with you. That means a master menu. When planning a menu, discuss your choices with the children. Ask their advice for dishes you may not have thought of.

On the other hand, if you can hop into the car to go shopping every day or two, take the young cooks with you, especially if they can buy foods that they'll later cook.

OLDER CHILDREN

For older brothers and sisters, plan foods that they can cook, or let them prepare some of the following dishes, being careful to make certain they understand the recipe. And, oh Mom and Dad, forgive me, but—don't hang over them while they're cooking. Be circumspect. Stand at least 2 feet away.

ABC SOUP

4 bouillon cubes dissolved in 4 cups warm water

1 potato, peeled and cut into small pieces

½ cup celery, washed and cut into pieces

½ cup carrots, washed, scraped, and cut into slices

1 tablespoon dried onion flakes, soaked for 10 minutes in

a little water

1 cup alphabet noodles

1. Pour bouillon into large pot, add potato, celery, carrots, and onion, and simmer for 15 minutes.
2. Add noodles and simmer another five minutes, or until noodles and potatoes are tender.
3. Serve and enjoy.
4. Properly dispose of vegetable peelings.
5. Clean up and put everything away.

STIR-FRIED CABBAGE AND CARROTS

1 small head green cabbage

1 large carrot

1 tablespoon olive oil

1 teaspoon salt

1 teaspoon sugar

1 teaspoon sesame oil

1. Slice cabbage into strips, as if you're making cole slaw.
2. Cut carrot into thin strips.
3. In large pot, add olive oil and heat.
4. Stir in cabbage, carrots, salt, sugar, and sesame oil.
5. Stir-fry for two minutes, or until everything is tender. Serve.
6. Properly dispose of vegetable peelings.
7. Clean up and put everything away.

B R O C C O L I   S T E M S

2 cups broccoli stems (left after flowerettes are used in other recipes)

1 teaspoon salt

1 tablespoon oil

1 tablespoon sesame oil

1. Peel the stems with a vegetable peeler, then cut them into thin slices.
2. Sprinkle with salt.
3. In large pot, add oil. Heat, and stir-fry broccoli for two minutes. Add sesame oil and serve.
4. Properly dispose of vegetable peelings.
5. Clean up and put everything away.

CHAPTER 4

Under Way

"Every age has its pleasures, its style of wit, and its own ways."

Nicoles Boileau-Despreaux, 1636–1711

WHEN ARE THEY OLD ENOUGH?

At what age are children actually ready for the great family outdoor adventure—whatever form it may take? Parents, of course, are the final judges of the age at which their child may be involved in an activity, though the tendency among proud moms and pops is to overestimate how ready their own children are. So here's a summary of recommended minimum ages that may help you evaluate your own children.

Canoeing: Kids under age six are basically guests only. We did meet one couple on a canoe trip in the wilderness of northern Quebec who had a year-old baby with them.

Six-year-olds can sit in the bow by themselves and actually do a bit of paddling with short, ultralight plastic paddles. But it really is the parent in the stern who does the work.

Nine-year-olds are ready to paddle the bow consistently for fair distances: quite capable of handling the stern—with proper instruction—in Class I water. With experience, can paddle bow or stern in mild white water. By age 10, active canoeists should have no problems on a lengthy canoe trip. However, parents must judge the weight they can carry on portages.

Rafting: Commercial raft organizations recommend a minimum weight of 50 pounds so the child can fit securely in a life jacket; must have the strength to hold on to a rope while the raft is bouncing through serious rapids, and the nature not to panic if something goes wrong.

Mountain biking: Most nine-year-olds have the skill and strength to handle day trips on relatively easy mountain trails; child should be at least 4 feet, 8 inches tall to fit the smallest fat-tire bike frames.

A group of young hikers on a family outdoor program sponsored by the Appalachian Mountain Club. Photo by Jerry Shereda.

Cross-country biking: Eight-year-olds with a multispeed gear bicycle should have no trouble covering 25 miles daily on paved or smooth country roads while toting their share of gear in a pannier and day or backpack.

Backpacking: By age five children can carry their own small packs and have the maturity to "keep moving"; they tend to get excited about little things close at hand, rather than enjoying the sweeping vistas that adults do on the trail.

High-altitude backpacking: At 8,000 feet or higher, the generally suggested minimum age is about 10 for moderately strenuous climbs. Above 10,000 feet, both adults and children will acclimate to the altitude far better if they relocate their camp no higher than an additional 1,000 feet each night.

Scuba diving and snorkeling: Eight. Swimmers should be taught both skills only by professionals.

Rock climbing: Eight to 10 on short, beginner cliffs. Learning, which involves the use of climbing hardware and ropes, is safest on indoor climbing walls under the supervision of climbing experts.

Campground (car) camping: No age restrictions.

Winter camping: Kids must usually be around six before they have the maturity to accept the inconveniences of a snowy winter weekend in a tent.

Snowshoeing: Six; need sturdy leg muscles and dexterity to manipulate plastic snowshoes.

Cross-country skiing: Six-year-olds can handle a few inches of snow on reasonably level ground.

Common sense suggests that children be given frequent breaks during any long-distance activity. Even the army gives troops on the march regular rests: 10 minutes every hour.

WHERE TO START

For an easy start take first-timers for a one-day trip, with a stop for lunch; they should carry some weight in the same pack they'll tote on future wilderness treks, whether by foot, bike, or cross-country skis. A long stretch of abandoned railroad track converted to recreational use could be ideal. To locate any in your area contact the Rails-to-Trails Conservancy in Washington, D.C. at (202) 797-5400.

CANOEING

Among the more joyous times for children are when they go canoeing, whether as wriggly young passengers with Mom and Dad who do all the paddling, or as canoeists or kayakers not only old

After a day or two on the water: "Hey, Mom, how do you like the way I'm paddling the bow? Great, huh!"

enough to handle their own vessels but also quite willing to show their parents how good they really are.

To appreciate such an activity with your kids it's really important that both adults and older children have some knowledge of paddling techniques—even if you only intend to pitch your tent on the shore of a lake and paddle to hidden corners of the waters before returning to your campfire for the night.

Basic skills can be acquired in a few hours of competent instruction and a couple of days of practicing what you've learned. Crucial are the key bow and stern strokes, so that the canoe goes where its paddlers want it to go, when they want it to go there, along with an understanding of why a canoe behaves the way it does.

Where do you find such instruction? In an astounding number of places. Most of the couple of thousand canoe liveries in the United States and Canada hold occasional training sessions for their clients. Virtually every one of the hundreds of canoe-kayak clubs has training programs. These may range from elemental skills to acquiring the superb control necessary to handle mean Class III white water—

rough, fast, and filled with foam and rocks. American Red Cross chapters offer occasional basic canoe training programs. And there are several dozen outstanding commercial paddle-kayak schools that offer weeklong paddling instruction at every level. Many advertise in *Paddler* and other outdoor magazines.

One of the pleasures of virtually all training programs is that they welcome young paddlers along with their parents—sometimes in the same session, sometimes with other juniors.

CANOES, PADDLES, AND PADS

It is estimated that more than 80 percent of canoeists rent their canoes, equipped with paddles and life jackets, from liveries. Let's take a quick look at what comes with a rental canoe, whether hired for a one-day casual trip on the waters of a gentle nearby river, or for paddling the remote and lonely waters of a northern Canadian province for two weeks.

There is one absolute for all canoeists: a properly fitting life jacket, otherwise known as a PFD (personal flotation device). The most popular are what the U.S. Coast Guard designates as the Type II and Type III. The Type II is shaped like a sort of horse collar that fits over the head; there's some support material around the back of the neck, but the bulk of it is across the chest. These will support an unconscious person face up. The Type III looks much like a down vest, with flotation material encircling the torso. It will not hold an unconscious paddler's head above water. Both adult and children PFDs come in a variety of sizes.

The only PFD recommended for children and nonswimmers of any age is the Type II horse collar. Since a life jacket can slip over a small child's head in event of a fall, it must be fastened with a cinch strap, which goes between the child's legs.

Look carefully at a rental PFD. Make certain the zipper fastener works properly and that the PFD itself fits comfortably and securely. An ill-fitting PFD not only cost one major livery on a popular canoeing river several million dollars in a lawsuit, but the life of the man who wore it.

PFD with padded shoulders, excellent for resting a canoe on when portaging. Courtesy L. L. Bean.

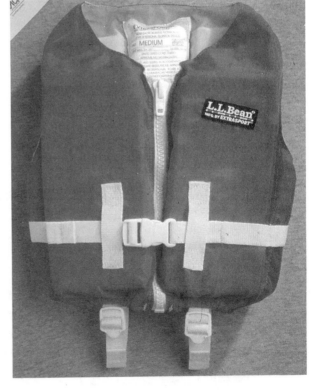

A child's PFD, showing the crotch straps which tie to the vest, preventing it from slipping off a small child. Courtesy L. L. Bean.

When there are little ones in a canoe, life jackets should be the horse-collar style, which will support the body with the head up and above the water.

The paddler, a novice canoeist, was among a group of cheerful friends off for a one-day trip. At the put-in, they were tossed paddles and PFDs by a careless livery employee. One man complained that his PFD seemed extra tight; could he get a larger one? "Naw, you don't need it man," he was told, "just tie it with the straps and don't worry about the zipper."

The paddlers climbed into their canoes and started off. Within an hour, the novice and his partner capsized. The man, a non-swimmer, drowned. He had been handed a large child's PFD that could not support his weight.

CANOES

Although superb aluminum canoes are still being made, livery operators today favor 16- to 17-foot tough plastic canoes. These are excellent—but they weigh in at 70-plus pounds, a ponderous weight when it must be carried, whether from a cartop to the water, or on a mile-long portage around a violent set of rapids. Unlike aluminum, plastic canoes retain their shape even if smashed into a rock. They also slide off rocks more easily, and make far less noise when banged into one. Why, your paddling friends may not even know you slid across the top of a rockopotamus when you are in a plastic canoe.

On wilderness trips that involve portages, veteran paddlers may opt to pay the extra rental fee usually charged for a light, sturdy canoe made of Kevlar, a material five times as strong as steel. A 16- to 17-foot Kevlar model will weigh about 45 to 50 pounds.

There's an ancient adage among paddlers who rent equipment: All paddles for adults are either too long or too short.

Only paddles for juniors seem to fit properly. Not to worry.

If in doubt, a bow paddler should get one on the slightly short side, a stern paddler one a bit long. And put a spare paddle into the canoe in the event of an emergency.

When you and your family reach the level of experience that allows you to take lengthy wilderness canoe trips, everyone should already own his or her own paddle and PFD. And, of course, when you buy PFDs select only those in vivid red or yellow. These are more easily spotted either when you must search for them before resuming your paddling adventure after a tasty snack ashore, or in a water emergency.

CANOE ACCESSORIES

Carry in each canoe a bailer made from a 2-quart plastic bottle with the bottom cut off, along with a large sponge. The bailer is a quick way to get rid of water that splashes, or rains, into the canoe. The sponge is for housecleaning.

Every canoe also should carry a painter—the canoeist's term for a 15- to 25-foot length of rope that is fastened both to the bow and inside the canoe. It can be used for everything from tying a canoe securely at night to making a ridge pole for a tarp or clothesline. Best: 3/8-inch floating polypropylene with a breaking strength of at least 2,500 pounds. This strength may be critical if you're trying to free a loaded capsized canoe lodged against rocks in fast water.

Waterproof bag from Northwest River Supply.

On weekend trips pack food either in ice chests or plastic 5-gallon paint or compound drums with tight-fitting lids. All gear that goes into a canoe should be tied to a thwart, whether it's the ice chest or a bag of spare clothes or personal items each person takes along. On longer trips, use sturdy camp bags with a single shoulder strap for food. These are much easier to shift around to attain proper storage and balance than are chests, drums, or those large, uncomfortable, ungainly wannigans, which our paddling forefathers carried in their wood-canvas canoes.

On weekend adventures, personal gear and clothing may be stuffed into a plastic garbage bag and tied to a thwart, or loaded into a backpack. The latter are not waterproof and should be lined with a garbage bag. On long trips the most satisfactory personal packs are those made specifically for the waterborne. An outstanding waterproof bag is a top-loader made of dacron coated with PVC, from Northwest River Supplies of Moscow, Idaho. It has shoulder straps for carrying on a portage or around camp, straps to hold the folded top secure from water, and short straps for pulling or pushing the bag around in the canoe or tent.

Waterproof canoe bags come in various sizes. A 2-cubic-foot bag is generally large enough for one person; a 4-cubic-foot bag will hold gear for two.

You can use a poncho to cover gear in the canoe in event of rain, or to spread out as tablecloth when you stop for lunch. Warning: Do not wear a poncho as rain gear. In the event of an upset, the poncho may entangle your feet. Instead, select a rain suit. And here's a hint: It's easier to hold rain suit pants up with suspenders in the twisting and shifting that goes on while paddling than it is with the thin tie belts that the pants usually come equipped with.

On pleasant sunny days, almost everyone wears shorts, exposing the thighs to the direct burn of the sun. Keep them covered with sunscreen.

As when you're skiing, bright sunlight not only hits you from above in a canoe but is also reflected off the water. Everyone should wear sunglasses—use only the type that block UV rays—and a wide-brimmed hat to shade the eyes.

CANOE SHOES AND SANDALS

In a canoe you have the options of wearing a snug, tight-fitting sandal with adjustable straps that secure the heel and the toes (so the sandals are not pulled off if you accidentally step into swift water or yucky mud), and slipping into old tie-on tennis shoes (which are cheap, shed water quickly, and are highly suited for casual paddling both for adults and kids). However, neither sandals or raggedy tennis shoes are suitable to wear around a camp or on a portage; those are places for comfortable outdoor boots. An ankle-high boot is more satisfactory for the canoeist than a low-cut only because of the muck and mud you often encounter getting into or out of your canoe.

Recently introduced is an ankle-high lace-up river shoe made by Patagonia. It has a quick-draining mesh, synthetic leather around the toe and heel, and a neoprene ankle to keep sand out. It also has a specially formulated sole for hiking on a rough, muddy, or steep slope.

In cold weather, shoes and sandals can be worn with wool or polypropylene socks to keep the feet warm. Or you can wear "wet suit" booties—which are fine in a canoe, but not ashore.

CLOTHING

Above all, especially for children, is the need to wear appropriate clothing. Except in warm, sunny weather when paddling warm waters, the most useless fabric for the canoeist is cotton. Repeat: cotton. When wet it has no capacity for holding in body warmth. Dress in wool or the synthetics designed to help the body retain heat even when soaking.

In cold weather canoeists wear wet suits, generally made of neoprene, that look like tight-fitting long johns. These retain heat because the neoprene cells, when wet, fill with water and are warmed by the body. New on the market are wet suits made of Polartec Thermal Stretch. The material is coated with a waterproof, breathable outer layer. The inner layer is a soft, microporous, water-repellent fabric. Perhaps the most significant difference between Polartec and neoprene is that the former has a warm fleece next to the skin—where neoprene feels slimy.

GETTING STARTED

One-day canoe trips, or weekend paddles that involve an overnight camp, are the optimal method of introducing the family to the joys and pleasures of canoe camping. The first consideration must be water safety. And this is established as much by example as by lecture. For example: Show your kids that they must wear their PFDs by wearing yours.

I have often seen adults not wearing PFDs insist that the children wear theirs. Are these the same motorists who yell at the kids to buckle on their safety belts while they drive bravely on without theirs? One glorious late-spring day, we were casually canoeing the federally protected Wild and Scenic section of the beautiful Delaware River when we came upon a canoe in serious trouble:

lodged against a rock, half full of water. The father, without a life jacket on, was standing in rushing water, struggling to get the canoe free. In the canoe was a boy of perhaps seven or eight, wearing his.

We instantly made an eddy turn downstream of the rock and swung our paddles hard to get to them. It took us several minutes to work the canoe free, then maneuver it to a nearby shore. We waited while the father rolled the canoe over to empty the water. As the dad thanked us and got back into the canoe I said, in none-too-gentle voice: "I'd keep my life jacket on if I were you. What would happen if you drowned in an accident? What would your boy do?"

"Sure," he agreed sheepishly. "I should."

We waved and paddled off.

An hour later, as we paddled through another fast stretch of water, I spotted the same canoe. Same dad. Same kid. Only one had his PFD on. It was not Dad.

WATER SAFETY

When you stop for a swim, insist that the young ones keep their life jackets on—even in shallow water. A mild river current can carry inexperienced swimmers much farther downriver than they intended to go. As for diving off rocks, check out the water to determine if it is deep enough for either diving or jumping into. Diving into an unseen rock can bring a swift end to a trip.

Older children who want to take a canoe for a paddle by themselves while the adults relax on shore should start off by paddling upstream or, on a lake, into the face of the wind. It may be quite a struggle for young paddlers to get back to shore if they start merrily on their way with the current, or the breeze, at their back, only to face the difficulty of returning against it.

It should not even be a matter of discussion that all the senior members of every canoe trip must be trained in how to resuscitate a drowning person, by either mouth-to-mouth or other forms of artificial respiration. Such training is almost universally available through the American Red Cross, the YMCA, local visiting nurse associations, and many canoe clubs.

In rainy or chilly weather, or after a fall into cold water, it is entirely possible for a paddler to develop hypothermia. Slender or thin people are the most susceptible. The first sign of hypothermia is excessive shivering, followed by an inability to paddle or even walk, and finally a lapse into unconsciousness. If possible, get the victim into dry clothes and wrap him or her in warm blankets. Start warming the torso—not the arms or legs—immediately. Cover the head and apply warmth to the back, under the armpits, and to the stomach. The packaged chemical hand warmers in your first-aid kit (see page 144) are an instant source of warmth. Hospitalization should be effected as soon as possible, because metabolic abnormalities are common after significant hypothermia.

WILDERNESS CANOEING

With the experience of easy one-day and overnight trips behind them, the paddling family is prepared to head for more remote waters.

Go!

It is critical that, if you paddle as a self-contained family, you follow rivers and lakes suitable for you. Never put in on any trip without a thorough knowledge of what lies ahead. Essential and very detailed information can be obtained from outfitters and liveries that serve the waters you'll be canoeing. Almost all that operate in wilderness regions not only rent equipment and sell wilderness foods, but also offer group tours or supply trained guides to lead you on unknown waterways.

If you wish to do it on your own, talk to someone who has actually canoed the waters. Study the official Canadian or U.S. contour maps of your proposed trip. Read the details of hundreds of wilderness canoe routes in excellent guidebooks widely available in outing goods stores, especially REI, Eastern Mountain Sports, and L. L. Bean.

Let me specifically recommend *Paddle America: A Guide to Trips & Outfitters in All 50 States*, by Nick and David Shears. It lists the names of almost 900 liveries and outfitters, including a description of their facilities and the rivers, lakes, and/or wilderness areas they serve.

The authors offer impressive advice for canoeists using the services of any outfitter or livery for the first time. They recommend, for instance, calling ahead to make reservations. And when you have the outfitter on the phone ask some basic questions, such as whether you can receive paddling instruction if you need it. What are the water conditions? At what age do they accept children? Will you need to shuttle your own canoe? On guided trips are the guides experienced, mature, and, if licensed, by whom? The Shears suggest talking to two or three liveries or outfitters serving the specific wilderness or river that you want to paddle.

RAFTING

Rafting the fabled white-water rivers of America certainly is popular. There is no reason an outdoor-oriented family would not enjoy

Young paddlers enjoy a rafting trip.

the excitement, the thrill, the challenge of tossing and rumbling through mountainous rapids. Raft trips are organized, arranged, and run by outfitters that provide everything from the raft guide to the meals and even the tents. Someone else does it all. You and your family go as passengers.

But hey, guys, in a canoe it's all yours.

CANOEING

Taking lessons is certainly the quickest and most effective way to pick up paddling skills, from the basics to those necessary to handle rumbling, foaming Class III rapids. However, do not overlook the excellent information for beginning canoeists that you can acquire from reading canoe books and watching videotapes. Among the books: *The Complete Book of Canoeing*, second edition, published by Globe Pequot Press, P.O. Box 833, Old Saybrook, CT 06475.

BACKPACKING

Have no doubt. The first reaction to backpacking by the very young after 15 minutes on the trail is: "Carry me. I'm tired." After a few futile moments of you pointing out how beautiful it is to walk in the woods, he or she ends up in your arms or riding on your shoulders from time to time.

Have no doubt. In a few years your child will be leading the family's backpacking expedition.

Once you start backpacking with children you never give it up as a family activity, because of the pleasure it gives everyone. This pleasure, of course, increases as the children grow older and more experienced, and as their backs can—what a lovely relief—carry an increasing share of the weight that goes into the packs.

There are no precise rules telling you how old youngsters must be before they can go on the trail for day trips. Infants still in the diaper stage can be carried in either a front pack, nestling against Mom's or Dad's chest, or a backseat carrier. It's self-evident, of course, that a trail trip with an infant is not going to be very long,

With a high capacity backpack for Dad, a back carrier for Mom to carry the littlest one, and big brother trudging in between, the family is off for a weekend overnight trip. Courtesy Tough Traveler. © MacDonald.

or on very difficult terrain. However, parents who know a trail well might consider an overnight trip of limited mileage.

By the age of four or five, most children are quite willing to do some trail hiking on weekend backpacking trips, carrying a pack with a few of their own belongings stuffed inside. It's a lot more fun if there's a nourishing, tasty tidbit in the pack that they can dig for when they want.

When young children of any age are hiking along beside you, it's important not to overpush them. No trail trip should become an exhausting experience.

EQUIPMENT

The backpacking family has almost—but not quite—the same equipment needs as any camping family. The limiting factor: weight. Review chapters 2 and 3, on personal and community gear, and trim their equipment suggestions to the barest essentials. Some examples:

Tents: A sturdy four-season tent that sleeps four and weighs about 15 pounds must be carried by one person—and it's going to be much more burdensome than it would be for two people to each carry a three-season tent that sleeps two and weighs in at about 6 pounds.

Kitchen: Look at your planned menu. How many pots and pans must really go with you? Three? Okay, so you don't cook and serve everything at once. Make it two. But be sure the large pot will hold a quart of liquid for each person. A pancake turner? Quite useful. Kitchen knife? Nope. Not if each adult has a personal sharp knife. Dipper? For dipping, use a cup. Egg beater? Use a fork. Stir like hell. No one will mind the noise.

Tarp: More important if you have young children. You might consider either an ultralight tarp or an extra poncho.

Lantern: No. Take a candle lantern with some extra high-stearate candles.

Camp stove: Yes. Even if you plan only to cook over a fire—and carry a grill—take one, and fuel. In dry weather, open fires may be prohibited. It also may be needed in an emergency.

Food: There is a rich variety of lightweight, easy-to-cook foods that you can buy commercially or prepare at home. Look at some of the recipes in Chapter Three.

Portable saw: Easier to carry and as good for cutting wood as a hatchet and a lot safer too.

Packing up: Use the Gordon Bag System (see pages 60-64). Carry the appropriate items in the kitchen utility, camp utility, and food utility bags. Put each day's meals in their own small bag. As soon as you make camp have everyone put the bags they are carrying in one central location.

    Before the start of the next day's hiking line up all the bags and distribute them according to the muscle power of each back.

Personal gear: The usual rule applies: If it's not truly necessary, leave it at home. Do you really need to carry that extra shoelace?

Baby on board! Carter Notch, New Hampshire. Photo by Robert J. Kozlow, courtesy Appalachian Mountain Club.

EXTRA CLOTHES

Clothing is one of the most critical items for the backpacker. Even for those families who head for the trails on only the warmest of summer days, weather is changeable. Chilling storms can sweep in. It is imperative that children, so susceptible to hypothermia, have suitable cold-weather clothing, from underwear to an extra jacket, for just such a shift from the balmy to the shivery.

If the weather becomes too severe for paddlers, they can head for the nearest shore. Backpackers must always be ready to find a site, pitch tents, and sit out a storm. At such times a camp stove is a gift of the gods.

LET SOMEONE KNOW

If storms or other serious problems prevent you from returning when you told your friends you would, you will be eternally grateful that someone knows you're having extreme difficulties, knows the route you're taking, and will organize a rescue mission.

BICYCLE CAMPING

A bicycle can be as much a part of family camping as a pair of hiking boots or a canoe. If you have sturdy, multigear bikes for the whole tribe, it really is a rather simple task to outfit them for cross-country bike packing.

The first step is to find a mechanic. Bicycles on a long trip undergo a heavy workout. Before you start, take your bikes into a bicycle repair shop and have a knowledgeable mechanic check each one out. Wheels perfectly straight. Gears greased. Everything working properly. You won't want one of the bikes collapsing when the family is 20 miles from the nearest telephone.

At the same time, if you don't have the appropriate wrenches and tools to maintain the bikes, and the necessary pump and patches to take care of a flat, the mechanic is the person to help you pick out what you need.

Carrying Gear

Camping bikers, like hikers, carry equipment in packs. The key to an acceptable biker's backpack is that it must ride comfortably low on your back when securely fastened. Check out everyone's pack for bike riding.

Clothes, food, and sleeping bags can be carried in packs; tents and gear can be loaded into two panniers hanging from a rack over the back wheel. While some specialized bike packs can be fastened to the front wheel or handlebars, these are not recommended by experts, who warn that they can interfere with proper handling of a bike ridden by a youngster, especially in an emergency situation.

Next, everyone onto their bikes, with packs and panniers loaded, for a trial run on a quiet, fairly level backwoods route. A few hours of this will give Mom and Dad a reasonable picture of how well each person handles a bike, and the limits for speed and distance of the weakest cyclist.

After all the preparation, where will you actually go for a bicycle camping experience? Probably the best areas are state and national forests and parks, with their wilderness beauty. Maps of the road and trail systems and campgrounds are available through most headquarters. Excellent and detailed maps, guidebooks, and pamphlets are sold at outing goods stores.

While mountain biking, like Alpine skiing, is popular as a day sport, the specialized fat-tire mountain bikes are not designed for carrying gear. This means that you cannot rent fat tire bikes for mountain camping. For mountain bike camping, plan trips only on trails or terrain you can handle with your own bicycles, or peddle from campground to campground on local roads.

Personal Items

One of the little pleasures when biking is having water available that you can drink from the container through a plastic straw while pedaling.

Also, take a look at the shoes you'll be pedaling in. Satisfied? If not, check out the pedaling shoes at bike shops. Light ankle-high outdoor boots should be fine when in camp, even if you all plan a little day hiking.

A sturdy bicycle lock is essential. Try a cable ski lock. If the cable is long enough it can be looped through both wheels so an admiring stranger cannot make off with either one. Or lock two bikes together with one cable lock for the front wheels and a second for the back.

What else is truly important for each bike camper?

- A good helmet.
- A small colored flag that can be attached to a staff on the back of the bike when you're road riding.
- Reflecting straps that can be worn when traveling in rainy or misty weather, or at night.
- (It's your choice. The Koosy-Oonek is smiling.)

BIKE MAINTENANCE ON THE TRAIL

Don't ignore the problems that can develop without routine maintenance. Here are some points to consider:

- Make sure that your shifting is smooth. If it becomes a bit balky it may be because something is rubbing. Check it out.
- Start a trip only with tires in excellent condition.
- Maintain tire pressure.
- Take a look at your cleats. If they are worn you may need a new pair for proper pedal contact.
- Keep bikes clean. Mud, grit, and sand can create a mess. You should not only spray bikes down but also go after the tiny corners with brushes and sponges.
- Carefully oil whenever necessary, especially the drivetrain.

That just about covers the special needs of the biking family. Go. Have a joyous time. Don't take down the tarp and start pedaling until the sun comes out.

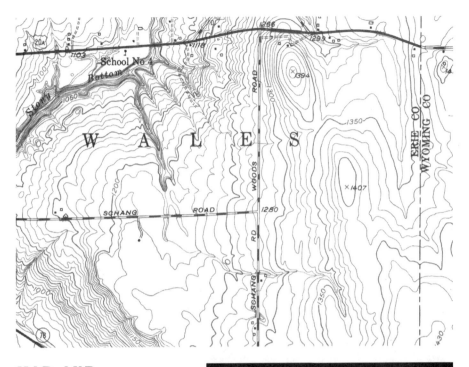

MAP AND COMPASS

It is sheer folly to head off on any wilderness trek with children, whether on marked mountain trails or rolling rivers, without a knowledge of contour maps and compasses and how to use them. First of all, a contour map is an instant, and accurate, drawing of a specific section of land. "Reading" its contour

What a Map Tells You

Contour lines: each line is exactly the same elevation above sea level. On this map major lines, in dark, are 50 feet above or below the next major line. The elevation for each major line is shown. The closer the lines, the steeper the slope.

If you are hiking from Route 78, lower left-hand corner, to the peak marked X1407, you will hike from about a 930-foot elevation to a 1,470-foot elevation. The distance is about 1.5 miles. If you are hiking at a rate of 3 miles an hour, this particular trip will take one hour instead of one-half, because every thousand-foot change in elevation adds one hour to your travel time.

lines tells you not only where a river bends or how the trail ahead is shaped, but also the conformation of the mountains and the rise and fall in a trail. And the compass tells you how to place the map so that it is accurately aligned with the terrain.

A World War II military-style floating needle compass. The compass housing has an "eye piece" and sighting "wire" for accurately determining the azimuth, or direction, to a distant object.

Whether or not I have a guidebook of the trail or river I choose to follow, I start our family wilderness trips by buying and studying two sizes of official United States Geological Survey maps of the area. One map is a small-scale, 1:250,000 series, in which 5 miles on the ground equals 1¼ inches on the map. This gives you an overview of a fairly large region. The other is a large-scale, 1:50,000 series in which 1¼ inches on the map represents 1 mile on the ground and clearly shows in great detail precise information about our route.

Next, sitting at a comfortable table at home, I take a piece of string 10 to 12 inches long and, measuring it against the mileage scale at the bottom of the map, make a mark every 3 miles on the river or trail we'll be following. When we are under way, a simple glance at the map and the terrain lets me quickly and accurately judge the distances we have yet to travel to reach a campsite, or have already covered.

While at the security of my table marking distances I also make special notations on the map of where to go in confusing areas. For example, if we'll be paddling a river flowing into a large lake covered with islands, with two or three places that look like outlets, we may have a major problem figuring which outlet is the correct one if it's a windy, miserable day. In this case I'll mark on the map itself the direction in degrees of the correct outlet. Lo, on the water I'll need only a glance at my compass to know if we are heading in the right direction or lost in the fog.

This same system saves just as much time and effort while backpacking. Several trails may cross each other, for instance; you must be certain the one you're following is the one you want. It's a wee bit disconcerting for a tired family hiking up a steep incline to a campsite to check the compass and find they should be on an azimuth of 90 degrees, not 150. Okay, back to that last intersection of trails, everybody. And try smiling.

Even if you are only vaguely familiar with map and compass, it will be illuminating for you to practice using them on easy, well-known trips when you always know within 10 yards where you are. Purchase a 1:50,000 USGS map of the area. Orient the map by aligning its magnetic north arrow with the north arrow of your compass. Practice locating yourself on the map by conspicuous visual landmarks. Then see how well you can actually find the direction to any of the landmarks in degrees. What direction or directions will you need to follow to reach your destination?

COMPASS STYLES

Compasses come in two styles. One has a needle on a minute post above a dial; the needle always points to magnetic north. The other is a floating dial compass in which the north arrow is painted on the dial itself. Virtually any compass will serve to keep a map properly oriented and will give you tolerably accurate directions in degrees to visible and distinctive landmarks.

Map and Compass

Teach your children as soon as they are old enough to understand what a compass is and why it's important. The first lessons should focus on the needle.

Pointing north. From that level, depending on their age and understanding, move on to advanced instruction. What is a map? What do the arrows in the lower right corner of the map mean? Get a large-scale topographic map of the area where you live and show the kids that it's actually a drawing of their neighborhood.

While directions can be given in such broad terms as north, south-by-southeast, or northwest, today they are more accurately given in degree. The direction by degrees is called the azimuth.

If you are a complete novice at using a map and compass, I recommend two instruction books. One is *Be Expert with Map & Compass*, by Bjorn Kjellstrom. It is available through the American Canoe Association Book Service, 8580 Cinderbed Road, Suite 1900, P.O. Box 1190, Newington, VA 22122. The other is *Maps and Compasses, a User's Handbook*, by Percy Blandford, available through the Appalachian Trail Conference, P.O. Box 807, Department SD, Harpers Ferry, WV 25425; (304) 535-6331. Both books are also widely available in bookstores.

Kids in Camp

"The days may come, the days may go,
But still the hands of memory weave
The blissful dreams of long ago."

George Cooper, 1838–1927

WILDERNESS ACTIVITIES

There are some wonderful activities to keep youngsters active and interested in the outdoors on quiet days, or in quiet moments. Consider how some of the following will fit into, or expand, your children's interests.

Diaries keep memories alive. So do photographs. Encourage older children on a family outing to use both. Younger ones may need a bit of extra help.

The secret of a fascinating diary that covers the outing is the daily entry. Since the young among us tend to forget or lose such things as a notebook and pen, perceptive parents will, naturally, have some extras inside their tent. For the preschooler, Mom or Dad does the writing. But the youngster does the talking.

Ask questions about the day: What was the most interesting thing that happened? Did you see any funny bugs? What did you like best about the breakfast? Where did you find all of that wood? Write it down—in *their own words.*

I know from personal experience that years from now, even when the tiny diarists have young campers of their own, the camp diary will always provide a wonderful trip down a memory lane that may have followed a river, or wound through the trees.

PHOTOGRAPHS

A diary can be enhanced handsomely through pictures.

Even the youngest in the family will find joy in taking pictures with an "aim-and-shoot" camera. But this comes about only when children are encouraged to take more than a few pictures of each other, or the Grand Canyon, or Old Faithful erupting skyward.

They can have fun putting their own campsite under study. Take pictures of tents being erected, food being cooked, someone building a fire, or hunting for frogs in the nearby pond. When the camp portrait is brought back from the developer, don't look and then drop the prints into the envelope to disappear forever. Albums are inexpensive.

Cameras can enrich a kid's camping experience. Cassie Cummings photograph.

Cameras also are of inestimable value in teaching kids about the flora and fauna of the wilds.

For example: Have them use their camera to study plant life. Take photos reasonably close to different flowers. If no one can identify the prints when you return home, head for the Internet or a good book on wildflowers so the kids will learn to recognize them through the photographs the young Ansel Adams took. Then put the prints in an album with the name of the photographer, the date each picture was taken, where it was taken, and the name of the flower carefully noted.

How about learning trees through photographs? Tree identification will require several different shots for the same tree, such as:

- A photograph of the entire tree to show its general shape.
- Shots of individual leaves.
- Closeups of the bark of the tree.

With prints back from the shop, let the tree photographer make up a small album of prints, similar to the one he or she made for flowers.

Mushrooms are worthy of photographic study. When taking a picture of one it will help with later identification if an object of known size is shown next to the mushroom, such as a hand or a coffee cup. If the mushroom is growing in an area too difficult for a good "portrait," remove it carefully, including the full stem, and carry it to a better area for its picture. Shoot one full side view of the mushroom, one straight down at the top, and—very important for identification purposes—one of the underside of the cap.

On a cross-country ski trek, the camera itself is eager to have its young keeper find and shoot snow prints left by birds, deer, and rabbits. Say, maybe that's the footprint of a *wolf!* For the best detail shoot the footprints at a slight angle, not straight down. Can the photographer identify the footprint when you get home?

The only limit to subjects studied for later identification is the imagination of the photographer.

FOR OLDER KIDS

They want to roam. They want to do. So how about bringing a copy of *Basic Mountaineering,* published by the Sierra Club, with its advice on how to climb the rocks and cliffs?

Or send them off to pan for gold. The U.S. Department of the Interior has a publication titled, "How to Mine and Prospect for Placer Gold," which has an excellent chapter on gold panning (Bureau of Mines, Information Circular 8517, available through the Government Printing Office, Washington, DC 20402). A few flecks could pay for your vacation. A few more for their college education.

It is quite easy to capture three-dimensional footprints of birds and animals if you bring a box of plaster of paris. Sprinkle a footprint in firm soil with about ½ inch of powder, spray lightly with water, and let sit until it hardens. Or make a thin solution of plaster of paris and pour it carefully into the print. Do not remove until it is hard.

FOR YOUNGSTERS

Bring a few small items—toys, games, a favorite picture book—plus, of course, their favorite blanket for sleepy moments.

CAMPFIRE MOMENTS

These are the soft, treasured moments of a camp experience that are only, and always, in the memory. Add something special to each evening around the small campfire. Sing songs. Roast marshmallows. Make up a play. Snicker at jokes. Here are a few books that can enhance the evening: *Scary Stories to Tell in the Dark,* by Alvin Schwartz; the poems of Rudyard Kipling ("You're a better man than I am, Gunga Din") and of Robert Service ("A bunch of the boys were whooping it up in the Malamute saloon. . . ."); *The Little Riddle Book* ("How do you get into a locked cemetery? Use a skeleton key"). Or perhaps a book of O. Henry's robust western stories or *Bury My Heart at Wounded Knee,* by Dee Brown, for the older kids to read by camplight.

FAMILY HONORS

We're a society that enjoys bestowing honors upon those who reach a goal, whether the first person to climb Mount Everest or the child who draws the best picture of

No! No!

What does not belong in the out-of-doors? A boom box to shatter the penetrating silence of the night, or, God forbid, a portable television set or any piece of civilized junk from the world of cyberspace. Enjoy each other and the solitude of the wilderness. It needs no embellishment.

life in the first grade. We give the man or woman who becomes a military officer an insignia of rank, or achievement. We hand a diploma to the student who graduates from high school, and one to the student who earns a college degree.

Of course these awards and medals, diplomas and honors are handed out by others who judge us.

Let us now honor our children who have succeeded in learning something about our wilderness. But—you, the parent, are the judge and the award giver.

Here are several "awards" that you can hand to your children for participating in outdoor activities, mastering specific skills, or learning something about good conservation practices.

The requirements are suggested. Add to or subtract from them. Then you alone interpret how well your children have done.

When your children complete the requirements, make the award ceremony a very special event. It could be a candle-lighting ritual or one by the light of a full moon or in front of a campfire. The honor bestowed can be almost anything, from a handwritten "diploma" to a Sierra cup with the child's name and date carefully marked with red nail polish.

WILDERNESS WANDERER
(SUGGESTED AGES, 5 THROUGH 7)

1. Clear a site for a safe, small campfire. Explain why it is important.

2. Gather enough downed wood to keep the fire burning for a half

hour. Demonstrate an understanding of why it is necessary only to burn fallen branches and to keep the campfire small.

3. Help put out a campfire and clean the fire site.

4. Help put up, clean out, and take down a tent.

5. Sleep a minimum of seven nights in camp, of which at least one is under the stars.

6. Go on a 3-mile hike with family or friends while carrying your own lunch and water. Clean up any garbage you find.

7. Identify a wild animal or bird or insect and draw a picture of it.

8. Dispose of garbage properly and explain what you are doing.

WILDERNESS CAMPER (AGES 8 THROUGH 10)

1. Select a proper site for your tent and explain why it is.

2. Choose a safe area for a fire. Build a small cooking fire by yourself. Keep it burning for at least one hour. Put it out. Clean the fire site and cover it with dirt so it doesn't look as if a fire was built there.

3. Sleep in tents for at least 14 nights.

4. Explain what a compass is and how it works. Use a map to travel for 1 mile.

5. Plan a full day's menu—breakfast, lunch, and dinner for your family.

6. Prepare one meal for your family in which at least one dish is cooked in camp, either over a fire or on a camp stove.

7. Select all your clothes for a weeklong wilderness camping trip and store them properly in your own pack.

8. Recognize, and name, five different trees, five different plants, and five different birds.

9. Take a 5-mile hike carrying all your own food and water in your own pack. Clean up all the trail debris you find and take it out with you.

10. Explain why it's important to have state and national parks and forests. Explain what is meant by *conservation*.

WILDERNESS SCOUT (AGES 11-PLUS)

1. Sleep in tents for at least 21 nights.

2. Demonstrate the proper way to wash dishes without affecting the water supply. Explain why this is important.

3. Photograph either an area that has been damaged by poor conservation practices, explaining what went wrong, or an area that has been preserved from damage. Explain why you think it has been protected.

4. Write a letter to your local newspaper either praising good conservation practices that have helped protect an area you've visited, or warning that poor conservation practices are damaging an area you've visited.

5. Clean up a campsite, properly disposing of biodegradable items, and properly cleaning and taking out all other garbage.

6. Show the proper way to erect and take down a tent; how to seal seams; how to repair holes or tears.

Disabled

Parents with disabled children do the whole family a healthy and joyous favor by including them in outdoor activities. Specialists who work with the disabled strongly urge parents who may not have done so to take them camping so they, too, may relish the beauty of the wilderness.

7. Explain the importance of staying on trails when hiking or mountain biking.

8. Take a 50-mile one-day bike trip, or paddle in a tandem canoe, either as bow or stern with a partner, for 10 miles in one day.

CHAPTER 6

The Safe Camp

"Prayer indeed is good, but while calling on the gods a
man should himself lend a hand."

Hippocrates, 460–377 B.C.

FIRST AID

here is a significant difference between first aid and treating a medical problem in the wilderness. First aid is the temporary help you can give a sick or injured person until an ambulance or qualified medical personnel arrive. Wilderness medicine touches on actual medical practice because help may be hours or even days away. Unless he or she has studied wilderness medicine, the least that is required of a trip leader is a course in first aid. These are widely available through every chapter of the American Red Cross.

To put together your own first-aid kit, start with a waterproof box, clearly labeled with red crosses painted with nail polish. The first item that goes into it is: a first-aid guide. I recommend any of the following booklets: "Wilderness Medicine," by Dr. William Forgey, available from the American Canoe Association Bookservice, P.O. Box 1190, Newington, VA 22122-1190; "Mountaineering Medicine," by Dr. Fred Darvill, available from the Skagit Mountain Rescue Unit, Box 2, Mount Vernon, WA 98273; and "Emergency Survival Handbook," by the American Outdoor Safety League, available through the Appalachian Trail Conference, P.O. Box 807, Department SD, Harpers Ferry, WV 25425.

Second is: a pair of latex gloves, to be worn when treating an injury where there is blood.

To help you consider what else should go into your kit, here are the items we carry on a major family wilderness outing of a week or longer, especially when friends are traveling with us. When we're not traveling, the first-aid box sits atop our refrigerator for the usual household emergencies.

Sharp pointed scissors.

Two rolls of adhesive tape, one broad, one narrow.

Band-Aids. Bring plenty. Kids enjoy wearing the colorful bandage strips.

Adhesive butterfly dressings to hold together the edges of a wound that may have to be stitched by a surgeon.

Sterile 2-by-2 gauze pads.

A roll of 2-inch sterile gauze bandage.

A roll of 3-inch Ace bandage.

Moleskin to cover foot sores and blisters.

A hypo-hyperthermia thermometer, which registers temperatures from the mid-70s to the 100s. This is especially important when checking the temperature of a person suffering from hypothermia.

A few single-edge razor blades.

Tweezers. Those with a built-in magnifying glass are helpful when you're pulling out almost-invisible slivers.

Several large sewing needles for digging out big slivers.

Over-the-counter cold medication.

A tube of sterile Vaseline.

Toothache medication.

Pain reliever—aspirin, Ibuprofen, Aleve, Tylenol.

Sore-throat lozenges and a medication for colds.

A few swab sticks.

Fingernail clippers.

Safety pins.

Several Kotex pads. These are excellent as pressure bandages as well as for feminine hygiene.

A small plastic bottle of rubbing (isopropyl) alcohol for cleansing instruments or wiping skin clean.

Over-the-counter drugs to control diarrhea and constipation, and Benadryl to reduce reaction to insect bites.

Several packages of the chemical hand warmers used by skiers. These are instantly important in a case of hypothermia.

And, finally, a small unopened roll of paper towels, any brand. The paper is as sterile as a sterile bandage.

PRESCRIPTION DRUGS

In a wilderness situation it is necessary to have on hand certain prescription medicines—*and a complete description by the physician who prescribed them of when and how they should be administered.* Among these are:

An antihistamine for violent reaction to poisonous plants, insects, or food.

A broad-range antibiotic for treating major infection.

A prescription medication to induce sleep.

A medication to control hysteria.

An anti-exhaustion drug, in case it becomes critical to postpone rest in an emergency.

A strong pain killer.

A medication for treating eye infections or to reduce eye pain as a result of lengthy exposure to brilliant sun.

And drugs for treating major diarrhea or constipation.

It is especially important to talk to your pediatrician or family doctor before taking youngsters under the age of 12 on a wilderness outing. She or he may suggest medication specifically for your children.

As I mentioned previously, any adults involved in canoeing, winter camping, or cross-country skiing should be able to administer artificial respiration and treat hypothermia.

MOMMY, WHERE ARE YOU?

There's an old saw about a grizzled hunter who wandered through thick woods searching for a sign of deer. Late in the afternoon, he decided he'd better return to camp. There was only one problem: The camp was not where he'd thought it was.

Snakebites and Lawyers

We no longer carry a snakebite kit. Medical authorities say these are, in effect, virtually useless. The appropriate treatment: an antihistamine to control violent reaction to the poison, and getting the bitten person to appropriate medical treatment as swiftly as possible. Of the 50,000 or so bites by poisonous snakes reported annually, the great majority of victims recover with no, or modest, treatment. Fewer die from poisonous snakebites than are killed by lightning.

Now, for snakebites of a different, but even more dangerous kind, be careful of legal bites if you carry prescription medicine. Legal authorities suggest you should not offer it directly to a person who seems in serious need of it; if there is a critical reaction, you may be subject to a major lawsuit. If you believe a person could benefit, however, what our legal adviser suggests is this approach:

You: "When I have this problem I take a prescription drug my doctor has given me. If you want to try it, please help yourself." Only offer the prescription medication with a witness present to confirm that you did not give it to anyone, but simply said that you had it.

Damn, this is the result of living in a litigious society.

The next morning, as he crawled out from a pile of leaves, a couple of fishermen saw him and hurried over. "Are you the guy everyone's hunting for? Are you lost?"

"Lost—*me?* Damnit, *no.* I know where I am. The camp's lost."

Or, as a friend of mine would warn his kids when they were camping: "Listen. If you wander off and get lost, come straight back to camp."

It's not a joking situation, however, as you may know if you've ever been lost, even briefly, while in the woods. But if it's frightening for an adult, envision how much more appalling it is for a child to discover he or she is lost in a maze of woods and even the familiar tent has disappeared.

Panic can kill. Should you suddenly find that your real world has vanished in a nightmare of trees and branches and sun and paths wildly going nowhere, stop. Stand still. Take a deep breath, or two, or three. Your racing heart will slow down. Now you can begin to think rationally about what to do next.

It's helpful to prepare your children for this moment, too; by sitting around sometime and chatting about getting lost. The lessons will be a helluva lot more meaningful, though, if your children actually take a class in Keepalive 101 while camped outdoors.

The first lesson you give to your youngster about what to do if lost should emphasize: "Don't give way to fear. Sit down. Stay where you are. Think. What should you do? If you don't come back to camp soon, someone will come looking for you. Stay where you are." A child—or an adult—who understands this has virtually a 100 percent chance of survival. It's the person who rushes blindly around in terrified panic who's in genuine trouble.

Fortunately, the younger the child is who wanders off and fails to return, the more likely it is that he or she will be found reasonably close to the tent and within a comparatively short, if dreadful, period of time. By school age, though, children can run into real trouble as they go poking and investigating and exploring farther and farther from camp.

You Will Be Found

The most powerful fact every child must understand is this: "If you get lost, someone will come looking for you. No, you will not be punished for wandering away. You may not be found for a day or two, but *you will be found. People will be out looking for you.*"

Once the violent panic has subsided and the youngster has stopped to think, what should he or she think about? "First, don't wander very far searching for a familiar landmark or trail. It could only make your situation more difficult. Make the very spot you're standing on your new home base for a little while. Mark it. Lay a couple of sticks on the trail crosswise. Drop your hat on it.

"So maybe you've hung around your new home base now, and no one has come searching for you, and it's getting late. Maybe sunset. The next lesson of survival is to find a place to keep warm and dry." A hungry, dehydrated, cold child stumbling through the darkness is, after all, a prime victim of that killer, hypothermia.

At this point in the lessons, the whole family goes walking, talking, looking. Ask questions: "Where would you spend the night if you couldn't find your way back to camp? Look, over there. It's a big hole in the trunk of that tree. Can you crawl into it? If it's pretty chilly at night how would you keep warm? Of course, you'd scrape up arms full of leaves and cover yourself with them."

If there isn't a hollow trunk or even a hint of a cave to go inside, ask "What other alternative are there? Look for a steep depression in the ground. Could you sort of crawl down there and snuggle under leaves?"

Here's a classic technique I learned as a Boy Scout to keep warm at night if lost: Coat yourself thickly with mud. Does it work? A few years ago, the evening news had a story of joyful parents whose lost son survived a freezing night by plastering himself with mud from a nearby swamp.

After shelter, your kids should know, the next most important item is water: "If you have access to a spring, a stream, a swamp, you can survive with nothing else for a week, or longer. Without water, survival may not exceed three days."

As the family moves through the outdoor classroom, talk about water and where to find it. "Yes, you can drink that yuck if you have to."

OTHER SKILLS

An older child can learn other life-surviving skills, such as ripping off branches and leaning them against a large tree to form a sort of shelter. Or covering the opening of a small cave with branches.

Hunting for a place to survive also can take the form of a game. You're all on a short trek along the trail. Suddenly Dad shouts out: "You're lost. It's getting dark. Go find a place to keep warm for the night."

Getting lost in a dry, desert climate, where the temperature may soar above 100 degrees F during the day and drop 50 degrees or more at night, poses a different set of problems. While finding a cave, or other shelter, for the night is essential in the desert, it is equally important to avoid the sun during the day.

The lost child should stay in shadows when the sun is broiling its way across the sky: "Hide in the shade of an overhanging rock. Under some brush. But remember that whoever is looking for you may come flying over in a helicopter or small plane, or bouncing across the ground in an all-terrain vehicle. At the first sound of a motor, run out where you can be easily seen. Wave your hands, a hat, or a sweater so they can see you."

Children are never too young to learn what their parents consider practical boundaries for them. For the older children, this involves more than: "You can't go beyond that road." Even if they shouldn't, they probably will. So try another approach, such as telling them to ask permission to leave camp and tell you in which direction they want to go; what, if anything, they want to see; and how long before they'll be back.

Somewhere around seven years of age, children can be taught how to use a compass and read a simple map. "This is my first compass," says Dad. "You can use it when we're camping. Put it down flat on a piece of wood. Look? The little arrow always points to the north." The lesson proceeds from there on as complicated a scale as you want to pursue.

Many campgrounds in state and national parks and forests offer maps of the campground area that show landmarks, some outstanding attractions such as waterfalls, a few trails, and nearby roads. For canoe campers, the livery from which you rented your equipment usually has a very good map of the waters it services. These are quite appropriate for first lessons in using map and compass.

ANIMALS, PESTS, AND SUCH

For a person to get mauled, or killed, by a wild animal in the wilderness is so rare that any event

The Friendly Whistle

For the child who's going to do some exploring on her own, or with friends, emphasize that she must not wander away from camp without a whistle hanging around her neck. If she does get lost she may hear someone blowing a whistle and yelling her name.

That's when she puts the whistle to her lips and wipes the tears from her eyes.

instantly becomes national news. This does not mean it is senseless to worry about the possibility, though, any more than it is senseless to worry about getting clobbered by a lightning bolt. You should be aware of a few precautions that will help you avoid the (remote) chance of an accidental encounter with trouble. In other words, don't stand on top of the highest hill in a thunderstorm.

A handy whistle can be a life-saver if a child is lost in the wilderness. Cassie Cummings photograph.

When hiking on a remote trail, tell the kids to make noise. Sing. Whistle. Remember, you are walking through an animal's home territory. The less startled the animal, the less likely it is to launch an attack.

Be careful on sighting a moose or an elk. Usually these animals will move quickly away, but each has been known to attack a person for no particular reason.

BEARS

Keep your camp free of garbage—which not only may attract a hungry bear, but will certainly bring in bugs and mice. Fishermen should clean their catch well away from the campsite.

Take no food into any tent for any reason in known bear country. If a hungry bear comes snooping around he is not going to be dissuaded from tearing a tent apart to find the food just because it's not his tent. Small animals also have a discourteous habit of getting into tents to scrounge for tidbits.

There are two main techniques used to protect food from bears—hanging and stacking. We use the latter. We stack up the food sacks, cover them with a poncho, and pile all the pots and pans on top of the poncho. The theory is that if a bear comes snooping she will knock the pans over; when they will tumble down they'll scare her off.

In all the years I've gone camping I've only twice had a bear actually come into a campsite snooping for food. The first time I heard a wild clattering, quickly poked my head out of the tent, and, in the dim dawn, saw a bear running away from the pots and pans that had come tumbling down. The second time I heard the same clattering, poked my head out, and saw a bear running off—this time dragging a food sack with him.

When the camp came to life an hour later, I told everyone what had happened. We could see a couple of broken clusters of brush and, cautiously, started following what we thought was the bear's trail. It was. We found the food sack perhaps 100 yards from camp. It had been torn open. Only one package of goodies was missing.

Steve Thompson, the wildlife biologist at Yosemite National Park, says hanging food does not deter bears.

"They have elaborate schemes for getting food. One time-honored precaution, hanging bags of food from a rope high in a tree, is now seen as useless. Local residents call food bags 'bear pinatas.'

"The bears chew off the rope that has been attached elsewhere, or chew off the branch that is supporting the bag. If the limbs are small, they'll send the cubs out. If that doesn't work they'll just climb above the bags, launch themselves out of the trees and grab the bags on the way down."

His recommendation: carry food in sealed 8–inch in diameter PVC tubs which bears cannot carry off in their mouths.

Baby animals, whether fawns or cubs, are attractive. Watch from a distance. Never, but never, come between a bear cub and its mother. If anyone is eager to take pictures, use a telephoto lens, not an Instamatic.

Firmly warn children that it is an invitation to trouble to try to coax an apparently friendly bear or other wild animal with a tidbit held in their hand. She may snap fast and hard, possibly taking a finger or two along with the tidbit.

INSECTS

Other than wearing long pants and long-sleeve shirts and using insect repellent, there is little you can do to protect yourself against stings and bites. The greatest danger from insects is getting stung by a poisonous spider, or infected with Lyme disease or Rocky Mountain spotted fever from a tick. It is imperative that bodies of both adults and children be thoroughly inspected every night and ticks promptly removed. Spider stings can be relieved by Benadryl, or a stronger prescribed antihistamine.

If stung by a bee, pull out the stinger if it's left in the flesh. Wasps don't leave a stinger—just one helluva sting.

Those who do not recognize poison ivy or poison sumac are destined by fate eventually to suffer the pain of coming into contact with one or the other. For treatment, wash thoroughly with a strong laundry or hand soap, then apply a soothing calamine lotion. The poison does not spread from the blisters that develop.

A BATCH OF SAFETY HINTS

After 20 years as a Scoutmaster working with some of the liveliest kids you'll ever meet in the wilderness, and an almost equal number of years camping, hiking, skiing, and canoeing with equally lively youngsters from diaper age to early teens, I've been confronted with every safety violation anyone might have thought of. So take a few safety tips from me. Given the bright minds of your own youngsters, of course, they will discover at least one I've never heard of.

If it Itches

To ease the itch and pain from insect bites, poison ivy, or poison sumac, apply water. Hot water. As hot as the body can stand. Soak for at least five minutes. Relief generally follows shortly and will remain for up to eight hours. Now the kids don't have to scratch the night away.

- If you haven't done so, take a course in basic first aid. For the family on remote backwoods outings, add to that a course in wilderness first aid.
- No candles, matches, or camp stoves in a children's tent. Youngsters will sometimes light them.
- *Giardia* is spread far more often by oral/anal contact than by drinking wilderness water without pumping it through a filter. Keep a pot of water and soap handy to wash in after a cat-hole trip into the nearby woods.
- Build campfires downwind from the tents.
- Do not leave a hatchet lying loose on a woodpile. Have you ever seen one slammed into a kneecap?
- Teach children how to use a hatchet safely. Let them practice by chopping kindling for the fire.
- Teach children how to use a knife and how to pass an open knife to another person.

- No diving into unknown lakes or rivers until you've personally inspected the depth and hazards.
- No food, no candy, no tidbits in tents at night. Animals, enormous or miniature, may come snooping in.
- No matter where you camp, protect food from prowling animals, and the morning kindling from rain and dew.
- Always wear latex, never plastic, gloves when treating emergencies that involve blood. For severe bleeding, bind a wound only with a pressure bandage, not a tourniquet, and get professional help swiftly.
- Wear a PFD when canoeing—even in a swamp only 6 inches deep. Carry an extra paddle in each canoe.
- Youngsters should never be permitted to go exploring without notifying parents where they are going and when they will be back.
- Wandering explorers should carry a whistle.
- Use a sunscreen with a sun protection factor of at least 25 to protect young, and even older, skin from cancer.
- Everyone should wear sunglasses with a high UV protection factor. They will help keep eyes from developing cataracts.
- Apply insect repellent to clothing to protect against ticks infected with Lyme disease or Rocky Mountain spotted fever, as well as hungry mosquitoes and deerflies.
- Every inch of every body of every mom, dad, kid, and dog should be checked every night for ticks.
- If kids go off to paddle by themselves, start them upstream, or paddling into the wind. Getting back will be a lot easier.
- Don't overpush children on canoeing, backpacking, or biking trips. Know their limitations before you start.
- When erecting a tarp, make certain the top is higher than the sides. A tarp full of rainwater makes an awful splash.
- Never pitch tents where an unexpected rain might send a waterfall pouring down a slope into them.

- Everyone on a biking trip must wear a helmet.
- Teach your children how to identify poison ivy and poison sumac.
- On wilderness trail hikes make noise, talk loudly, and laugh to advise nervous animals that you are walking through their home territory. Scat.
- Buy only tents with a fabric specifically marked FIRE RETAR-DANT. They will burn. But they will not flash into flame with a single match.
- On long trail and canoe trips tell someone where you are going, your route, and when you will return.
- Add a few extra items of clothing to everyone's pack that will come in handy if there's a sudden change in the weather.
- Old car batteries sometimes fail when the car is left untouched for as little as a week. If in doubt rev up the engine every couple of days. Before driving off into the wilderness make sure your trunk has battery cables, a flashlight, a jack, and chains to get the car out of mud, sludge, or ice.
- Carry moleskin for the foot blisters that may crop up on trail trips. Especially for anyone wearing new hiking boots.
- Talk to your veterinarian about what your dog may need before taking her on a backpacking, or wilderness, trip.
- Paper towels are sterile.
- Rocks, leaves, sticks, or snowballs may cause major anal infections if used as a substitute for toilet paper.
- Drink plenty of water. Start every dinner with soup. Dehydration when you're physically active can cause nausea, irritability, and severe headaches, or even lead to hypothermia in damp, cold weather.
- The last thing at night: Inspect the camp to make certain everything is secure. Take the kids with you if they're still awake. When you're satisfied, smile, relax, then everyone off to their tents for a long, pleasant snooze.

CHAPTER 7

Where to Go

"Oh, I know where I'm going
And I know who's going with me."

folk song

In the magnificent open spaces that still comprise a grand chunk of America there are mountains to climb, rivers to paddle, and trails to backpack, and all are open to the family who relishes the glory of the outdoors. This section lists a number of the organizations whose members enjoy using and protecting our outdoor resources. Many sponsor outdoor activities for families—both the national organizations and their local chapters.

For the camping family there is no more pleasant way to meet other families who also relish going beyond the confines of city streets and sidewalks than to join one of these organizations. Some, like the Sierra and Appalachian Mountain Clubs, offer a broad range of activities, from fighting for national conservation projects to helping maintain hiking trails and to sponsoring family al fresco adventures. Others focus on one activity, such as the Adventure Cycling Association for those whose pleasure is pedaling scenic backroads and trails, or the National Speleological Society, which would rather explore the depths than climb the heights. Many clubs include programs for those with disabilities.

Here, by way of an example, are some of the outdoor activities for families sponsored by the New York–New Jersey chapter of the Appalachian Mountain Club, in the fall of 1997:

Family Walk to Long Island's Tallest peak (401' elev.). Leisurely pace, probably 3 miles round trip, for young children (recommend ages 4–8). Bring fun food and water. . . .

Family Sail. Join skipper and his 7-year-old son for approx. half day sail, w/instruction. Intended for never-evers or beginners who want to instruct their children (recommended age 5+) to the joys of sailing. . . .

Family Canoe Day Trip. Enjoy an easy paddle on this LI river near Northport. Children of all ages welcome with responsible adult. . . .

Family Outing in South Mountain Reservation. A very leisurely walk to a stream and followed by a waterfall. Will play along stream during lunch. Geared for kids 2 to 6 years old. . . .

Both Sierra Club chapters and the National Sierra Club run family outings. Chapter outings are typically weekend activities; longer trips are offered by the national organizations. Membership in the Sierra Club is not necessary to participate.

Here are several of the typical family programs sponsored by the national organization during the summer of 1997:

Fiery Furnace and Devil's Garden Family Adventure. Arches and Canyonlands Parks, Utah. March 30–April 5. . . . Short, easy day hikes make this a great way for young children and their parents to enjoy the outdoors together. Minimum age is 2. . . .

Children's Museum, Ritchey Woods Nature Preserve, Indiana, June 26–30. . . . Share the joy of the outdoors and volunteer to upgrade trails at the greenest part of the world's largest children's museum. Age-appropriate projects will delight participating children 6 and older. . . .

Vermont Preteen Hike and Bike, Groton Forest, Vermont, July 27–August 2. . . . We'll base camp in a circle of lean-tos alongside

Kettle Pond in Groton State Forest. Bike on quiet roads, hike to mountain overlooks, discover a bog. Activities are designed for families with children 8 to 12. . . .

Family Backpack, Big Basin Park, California. August 18–24. . . . We'll meet at Pigeon Point Lighthouse and return there after a 32-mile descent from the skyline to the sea, spending each trial night at a well-located camp. Suitable for children age 10 and up. . . .

Descriptions and details of all national trips, both domestic and worldwide, are listed in the Sierra Club's January-February issue of its bimonthly magazine, *Sierra*.

The family outdoor programs of—for example—the New York section of the Atlantic chapter ranged from easy day hikes to a weekend learn-to-canoe program for parents and kids.

Everybody comes along to the family camp.

GENERAL OUTDOOR ORGANIZATIONS

The following are among the better-known national outdoor organizations with family outing programs. All can send you information about their national activities and local chapters:

Adirondack Mountain Club, 814 Doggins Road, Lake George, NY 12845; (518) 668-4447; fax (518) 668-3746; http://www.adk.org
>   Encourages the use, as well as the protection of New York's wilderness Adirondacks. Publishes a magazine, *The Adirondack*.

Alpine Club of Canada, P.O. Box 1026, Banff, AB TOL OCO CANADA; (403) 762-4481
>   They love the mountains.

American Hiking Society, P.O. Box 20160, Washington, DC 20041-2160; (301) 565-6704; fax (301) 565-6714; e-mail ASHMM-BRSHP@ail.com
>   The magazine for members contains fascinating information for those who, actively or passively, enjoy the outdoors.

Appalachian Mountain Club, 5 Joy Street, Boston, MA 02108; (617) 523-0636; fax (617) 523-0722; http://www.outdoors.org
>   A conservation- and outdoor-oriented organization with a rich variety of family activities operated by local chapters.

Appalachian Trail Conference, P.O. Box 807, Harpers Ferry, WV 25425; (304) 535-6331
>   Chiefly concerned with maintaining and protecting the famed Appalachian Trail, which follows mountain ridges and forested valleys from Georgia to Maine.

Federation of Western Outdoor Clubs, 4534 University Way NE, Seattle, WA 98105

The Green Mountain Club, P.O. Box 889, Montpelier, VT 05601; (802) 223-3463
>   Major goal is maintaining and encouraging the use of the Long Path, a trail that bisects Vermont from north to south.

The Mountaineers, 300 Third Avenue West, Seattle, WA 98119;
(206) 284-6310

Their worldwide goal: the big ones!

Mount Rainier National Park Associates, 15242 Southeast 48th,
Bellevue, WA 98006

The Nature Conservancy, 1815 North Lynn Street, Arlington, VA
22209; (703) 841-5300

Vigorous interest in conservation.

New England Trail Conference, P.O. Box 145, Weston, VT 05161

Protecting and encouraging the use of trails in New England.

Pacific Crest Trail Association, P.O. Box 1048, Seattle, WA 98111

Protecting and encouraging the use of the Pacific Crest Trail.

Sierra Club, 730 Polk Street, San Francisco, CA 94109; (415) 776-
2211; http://www.sierraclub.org

One of the largest outdoor and conservation organizations in
the world. Chapters throughout the United States.

The Washington Trails Associations, 1305 Fourth Avenue, Suite 512,
Seattle, WA 98101; (206) 625-1367

Wilderness Society, 900 17th Street NW, Washington, DC 20006;
(202) 833-2300; www.wilderness.org

Major advocate of conservation programs.

CANOEING AND KAYAKING

American Canoe Association, 7432 Alban Station Boulevard, Suite
B232, Springfield, VA 22150; (703) 451-0141

Hundreds of canoe clubs throughout the nation that teach
canoeing and kayaking, organize river activities, and encourage
protection of the nation's waterways.

American Whitewater Affiliation, P.O. Box 636, Margaretville, NY
12455; (914) 586-2355

Encourages white-water paddling, river conservation, and river
access. Member clubs throughout the United States.

Canadian Recreational Canoeing Association, P.O. Box 500, Hyde
   Park, ON NOM IZO, CANADA; (519) 473-2109
   Affiliated clubs throughout Canada.

CAVING

National Speleological Society, Cave Avenue, (cq) Huntsville, AL
   35810; (205) 852-1300
   When you want to meet the guys and gals and youngsters who
   go down deep.

BICYCLING

Adventure Cycling Association, P.O. Box 8308, Missoula, MT
   59807; (406) 721-1776; fax (406) 721-8754
   The association has marked more than 20,000 miles of scenic
   backcountry and mountain roads for bicyclists. Maps and information on all the routes are available from the ACA.
Transportation Alternatives, 115 West 30th, Suite 1207, New York,
   NY 10001; (212) 629-8080; www.transalt.org
   Several national chapters. Strong advocates of protected bicycling routes in cities.

OUTDOOR ACTIVITIES FOR THE DISABLED

   Among the organizations offering activities that integrate the
disabled into regular outdoor programs are:

Environmental Traveling Companions, Fort Mason Center, Building
   C, San Francisco, CA 94123; (415) 363-2647
   Offers sea kayaking, rafting, and cross-country ski trips.
Whole Access, 517 Lincoln Avenue, Redwood City, CA 94061; (415)
   363-2647
   Many ski areas also provide special facilities for those with dis-
abilities.

TRAIL SYSTEMS

One of the splendid aspects of the Americans appreciation of the out-of-doors is the variety of hiking, backpacking, skiing, and bicycling trails that weave their way through every corner of our nation.

APPALACHIAN TRAIL

One of the most famous hiking paths in the world is the Appalachian Trail, 2,146 miles long, which runs from the scenic heights of Springer Mountain in Georgia along the Appalachian Mountain ranges to the rugged summit of Mount Katahdin in Maine. An estimated 4 to 5 million hikers walk some parts of it every year. Hundreds have trekked the entire trail, some over years, others in one continuous hike that takes about six months. Built by volunteers from 1921 to 1937, the trail is now protected by the federal government as a National Scenic Trail. For information, guidebooks, and maps, call the Appalachian Trail Conference.

RAILS-TO-TRAILS

Then there are the trails created by the Rails-to-Trails Conservancy. Its goal is simple: Convert every abandoned railroad line in the United States into a walking-skating-hiking-biking-cross-country-skiing-or-do-whatever route. The first project was the conversion of an abandoned 55-mile-long stretch of railroad now known as the Illinois Prairie Path. Today there are almost 10,000 miles of converted railroad beds, some in every state of the Union, ranging in length from a few to hundreds of miles. For information on rails converted to trails in your area contact the Rails-to-Trails Conservancy at 1400 16th Street NW, Suite 300, Washington, DC 20036; (202) 797-5400; www.railtrails.org.

The Rails-to-Trails Conservancy has transformed abandoned railroad beds into ideal cycling paths. This is the Cannon Valley Trail in Minnesota. Photo by Patricia Schmidt.

PACIFIC CREST

Following the crests of the Cascades and Sierra Nevadas from the Washington-Canada border to the California-Mexico border, the Pacific Crest National Scenic Trail runs for 2,608 miles from semi-arid desert to soaring mountain peaks. For information: Pacific Crest Trail Association, P.O. Box 1048, Seattle, WA 98111.

IDITAROD

An outdoor family needn't travel by dogsled to enjoy the lonely wild summer magnificence of the Iditarod Trail in Alaska, best known for the grueling long-distance sled-dog race held there every March. The trail originally connected mining camps and trading posts. For information: Iditarod Trail Committee, P.O. Box 87-0-800, Wasilla, AK 99687; (907) 376-5155.

CONTINENTAL DIVIDE

When completed, the Continental Divide National Scenic Trail will be the longest and toughest of the nation's growing scenic trail system. It will stretch 3,200 miles and range in altitude from 4,000 to 13,000 feet. For information: Forest Service, 11177 West Eighth Avenue, Box 25127, Lakewood, CO 80225-0127; (303) 236-9501.

Both state and national forests and parks are also crossed by trails of every degree of difficulty.

TRAIL MARKERS

One comforting part of hiking maintained trails is that they're generally marked on trees or boulders with a distinctive insignia every 50 to 100 yards. Where a trail goes through a civilized area, the markers also pop up on telephone poles, bridge girders, and sides of buildings. Hikers on the Appalachian Trail follow a white bar 2 inches wide and 6 inches long. Where the trail makes a distinctive turn, two bars are painted, one slightly above and to the left or right of the other. The trail follows the upper bar. Virtually all marked trails use this same signal or a turn: Two markers side by side mark the beginning or end of local trails.

Trail maps usually depict markers, which can be any distinctive shape or color.

A vast number of guidebooks and pamphlets with detailed descriptions and maps of both national and local trail systems are available in every outing goods store, and many bookstores, throughout the United States.

For information on specific U.S. Geological Survey contour maps of areas in which your family is interested, call the USGS at (800) USA-MAPS, or (800) HELP-MAP.

COMMERCIAL OUTDOOR ORGANIZATIONS

There are, quite literally, several hundred commercial organizations that sponsor a rich variety of excellent outdoor programs for families with children or, in some cases, simply for children both in the United States and other countries.

Consider, for example, what Rascals in Paradise, a San Francisco organization, does for outdoor families. It puts together groups of three to six families for trips it describes as: "Divers with Kids," in Honduras, Fiji, and the Bahamas; "Africa, the Real Zoo," for travel through central Africa; plus family trips to the Galapagos and New Zealand.

Arctic Treks, in Fairbanks, Alaska, offers family programs that include high Arctic base camps and day hiking trips in isolated areas reachable only by floatplanes.

The only fundamental difference between family trips sponsored by noncommercial organizations and those put on by commercial outfitters is usually the cost. But for those who can afford the latter, they are focused on active participation and deeply concerned with conservation and the environment.

Two outstanding guidebooks that describe these organizations and their programs in great detail are: *Great Nature Vacations with Your Kids,* and *Great Adventure Vacations with Your Kids,* by Dorothy Jordan. Contact World Leisure Books, 177 Paris Street, Boston, MA; (617) 561-7654.

Jordon's books also list numerous areas throughout the United States that offer sight-seeing and camping opportunities, a well as outdoor activities, summer and winter, for parents who wish to design their own programs.

WILDLIFE ORGANIZATIONS

Every outdoor family interested in the environment and the protection of wildlife should belong to at least one of the following:

Defenders of Wildlife, 1244 19th Street NW, Washington, DC
    20036; (202) 659-9510

Fund for Animals, 200 West 57th Street, New York, NY 10019;
    (212) 246-2096

Greenpeace USA, 1436 U Street NW, Washington, DC 20009; (202) 462-1177

Humane Society of the United States, 2100 L Street NW, Washington, DC 20037; (202) 452-1100

International Fund for Animal Welfare, P.O. Box 193, Yarmouth Port, MA 02675; (508) 362-4944

International Union for the Conservation of Nature and Natural Resources, Avenue du Mont-Blank, CH-1196 Gland, Switzerland; 022.64-91-14

Izaak Walton League, 1401 Wilson Boulevard, Level B, Arlington, VA 22209; (703) 528-1818

National Audubon Society, 700 Broadway, New York, NY 10022; (212) 979-3000

National Wildlife Federation, 1400 16th Street, Washington, DC 20036-2266; (202) 797-6800

The Wildlife Society, 5410 Grosvenor Lane, Bethesda, MD 20814; (301) 897-9770

World Society for the Protection of Animals, 29 Perkins Street, P.O. Box 190, Boston, MA 02130; (617) 522-7000

World Wildlife Fund, 1250 24th Street NW, Washington, DC 20037; (202) 293-4800

OUTDOOR GEAR AND CLOTHING FOR CHILDREN

Wildlife and Conservation

How to join a wildlife or conservation organization: Have each parent and each child sign up for a different one. Spread your support and money. They all are worthy.

Virtually every outing store in the country, and certainly every major department store or chain, offers an extensive range of summer and winter clothing, gear, and packs for children. When you're shopping you'll usually find the most accurate information at the outing goods stores. Here are a few:

Campmor, Box 700-T, Saddle River, NJ 07458-0700; (800) CAMP-MOR
   Excellent variety of whatever you are looking for. Catalogs.

Eastern Mountain Sports, One Vose Farm Road, Peterborough, NH 03458; (603) 924-6154
   National chain with outstanding clothing and gear.

JanSport, 10411 Airport Road, Everett, WA 98204; (800) 552-6776
   Noted for their quality packs.

L. L. Bean, Freeport, ME 04033; (800) 826-5767
   Even if you've never seen it—only thought about it—it's in this vast store. Catalogs.

Moss, Inc., P.O. Box 309, Camden, ME 04843; (207) 236-8368
   A line of fabulous tents. Now sold by REI.

Northwest River Supplies, 2009 South Main Street, Moscow, ID 83843; (800) 635-5202
   Everything for the canoeist and kayaker.

Recreational Equipment, Inc. (REI), Sumner, WA 98390; (800) 426-4840
   A national co-op outing goods chain with excellent merchandise for everyone from paddlers to mountaineers.

Tough Traveler,® Schenectady, NY 12307; (800) GO-TOUGH
   Products can be purchased through specialty dealers or by mail order.

Sierra Trading Post, 5025 Campstool Road, Cheyenne, WY 82007; (307) 775-8000
   Wide variety of discounted outdoor clothing. Catalog.

EPILOGUE

"Life consists with wildness. The most alive is the wildest. Not yet subdued to man, its presence refreshes him."

Henry David Thoreau, 1817–1862

It was a soft and pleasant day. The sun strolled casually into the late afternoon.

We had spent the day meandering along a nearby stretch of the Appalachian Trail, which terminates its cross-country journey from Georgia on the spiny backbone of Mount Katahdin, only a few miles from where we were camped in Maine's wild and forested Baxter State Park.

Our two daughters sat in front of their green tent waiting to see if any ground squirrels would come snooping around for the peanuts they'd scattered before we left camp. My wife, Gail, and I were quite content to sit at a sturdy, heavy wooden camp table and relax.

There were only a few other tents in the campground. A blue sedan rolled up to a neighboring site. The car stopped. Out leaped two young boys, perhaps six and eight, followed by their parents.

They carefully investigated the site, picking out places to pitch tents. Like us, they had two tents. One for the boys. One for the parents.

Photo by Robert J. Kozlow, courtesy Appalachian Mountain Club.

The boys, laughing at each other, had trouble getting the wands into the right holes for their self-supporting tent. Dad, a tall, quick-moving man with cheerful eyes, soon came over to give them a skilled hand, and in minutes their tent was erected and stuffed with their gear, which they'd hauled from the car trunk.

"It's getting late," my wife said.

"I'd better start the fire," I said. "Okay, girls. Work time. Go out and drag in some dead branches off the ground. We've gotta get ready for dinner."

"We're looking for squirrels," Rebecca said.

"Did you see any?" Hilary asked.

"Nope. But you might see some while you're getting kindling."

Off they walked. We paid little attention to their wood-gathering efforts.

While they were looking for twigs, the boys of our new neighbors walked over to watch them. Within minutes they, too, were gathering twigs and helping the girls bring them to our fire site.

We greeted them. They told us their names. They said their dad wanted to camp nearby because he saw the girls.

They said he liked to camp near other families. "So do we," Gail told them.

Dad strolled over to gather in his boys. We introduced ourselves. Herb; Pat. Friends are easily made in wilderness camps.

I invited them to join us for hot chocolate, coffee, a brandy, and marshmallows after dinner. We shook hands.

Gently the sky darkened.

DINNER

As the flames began to dance Gail laid out the food on the camp table. Dinner began with a store-bought onion soup enlivened with fresh minced onion. The girls played an active role in its preparation, measuring the water and helping sauté the onions before they were added to the soup pot. Twice during the time it took to broil a chicken carefully split into two halves, the two boys came over to talk to the girls—to ask what we were

eating, to tell us they were having a steak and some mashed potatoes from a box, to find out when they all should come over for
marshmallows. Twice their mother came over to drag them back.

"Can we go over and see what they're eating?" the girls wanted
to know. "It wouldn't be polite," their mother said. In a few minutes I walked over and brought them back.

It was quite dark when I told the girls it was time to invite our
guests. Take a flashlight.

They all came talking and laughing into our camp.

We sat around a small fire.

We drank coffee and hot chocolate, ate the cookies they'd
brought, roasted marshmallows. And the adults had a pleasant
drink.

I found Pat a warm, energetic sort who said, frankly, it was difficult for him to sit still. His wife said: "He's always busy."

The mothers scooted the children to their tents.

He and I talked.

As friendly strangers so often do, we shared some rather inti-
mate thoughts. We poured another drink. He said this was his
second marriage. "I lost my first wife and son because I was too
damned busy to do anything with them. Making a few extra dollars was my goal. I'm an accountant in a brokerage firm. Hell, I
never thought of going camping with my family then."

"What got you started?" I probed.

"My wife." He pointed to her as she stood in lantern light
straightening up their camp table. "I met her through a friend and
she invited me to go on a one-day hiking trip with a club she
belonged to. It was, really, my first time. When did you get started?"

"As a kid growing up in the mountains of southern Idaho. I've
always done this kind of stuff. Do you enjoy getting out?"

"Yeah, especially after the kids were born. It's a way to have fun
with the family, to enjoy doing something together, I mean something meaningful together."

We sat in silence. He got up and said good night.

I said we were going to take a "backpacking trip" the next day.
"Just going for a longer hike on the trail, carrying our own lunch,

and stopping wherever we feel like to eat before coming back to camp. Would you folks like to hike with us?"

"It would be a damned pleasure."

"Good."

And so the next day we again were on the Appalachian Trail, this time heading toward a lake adjacent to the trail considerably farther away than we had gone the day before. The kids were constantly ahead of us, the boys only slightly showing off how they were older, larger, stronger, and better hikers than the girls, and offering occasionally to carry their small packs. The girls refused.

That night, after dinner, we joined them for a campfire snack. Again, Pat and I sat around the fire embers for a nightcap after all the kids and ladies had retired.

We talked wilderness talk. Of lakes and hikes. Of trails we wanted to walk. Of mountains we would climb some distant day.

SUMMER PLANS

He asked what we planned for next summer—anything special? No, not until the girls are a bit older. Your plans?

"I'll show you," he said, and walked over to his car and brought back a magazine. It was that year's outing issue of the Sierra Club magazine.

"Look." He opened the pages to the section dealing with family outings. "We're going to go on one of these." The specific outing he pointed to was a week on a family service trip helping build a new trail in the Coconino Forest of Arizona.

He said: "I think we all should give something in return for the pleasure we get out of family camping."

INDEX

"How to Mine and Prospect for Placer Gold," 138
hypothermia, 122, 147
Hypothermia (Forgey), 76

insect repellent, 6–7, 153
Inside Outings (Benner), 79

Johnson, Dr. Wade, 48–49
Journal on Wilderness and Environmental Medicine, 79

Kella, Dr. John, 29
Kipling, Rudyard, 138
kitchen equipment, 2, 126
    accessories, 57–58; knives, 57; pots and pans, 55–57, 126; stoves. See stoves; tableware, 58
Kitchen Utility bag, 60, 62
knives, 3–4
    for cooking, 57; pocketknife, 59
Koosy-Oonek, 3, 37–39, 130

lanterns, 126
lost in wilderness, 145–149
lyme disease, 151, 153

maps, 41, 131–133
    of campgrounds, 129–130; 148; trail systems, 129, 163
Maps and Compasses, A User's Handbook (Blandford), 134
matches, 4
Medicine for Mountaineering (Wilkerson), 78
menus and recipes, 126
    breakfast, 89–91; and dining well, 81–83; dinner, 93–101; fast-cooking carbohydrate recipes, 101–102; golden oldies, 103–106; lunches, 92–93;

menus and recipes (*cont.*)
    meat and poultry, broiling, 57, 102–103
"Mountaineering Medicine" (Darvill), 142–143

National Speleological Society, 155, 160

On the Trail with your Canine Companion (Smith), 54
outdoor organizations
    bicycling, 160; canoeing and kayaking, 159–160, caving, 160; commercial organizations, 163–164; disabled, 160, national organizations, 158–159

Paddle America: A Guide to Trips & Outfitters in All 50 States (Shears), 122
personal equipment, 2–5, 126
    insect repellent, 6–7; outdoor clothing, 11–12; rainwear, 12–13; toilet articles, 5–6
poison ivy, 49, 151–152
poison sumac, 49, 151–152
pots and pans, 55–57, 126
    black pots, 60; Dutch oven, 57

rainwear, 13
rafting, 123–124
    and children, 111
Rascals in Paradise, 164
Rawlins, Dr. Bernard, 29
rock climbing, 112
rocky mountain spotted fever, 151, 153

saws, portable, 126
Scary Stores to Tell in the Dark (Schwartz), 138